Dear Guy &

This Book is Hard to

FOR THEIR TEARS I DIED

Get through, I knew, But it

opened my Heart and Mind

to the Problem of Human Sex

trafficking.

Love you Both,

Christina

STORIES OF EXTREME SUFFERING
AND EXTRAVAGANT REDEMPTION
IN HUMAN TRAFFICKING AND SOCIAL INJUSTICE

FOR THEIR TEARS I DIED

Patricia King • Shirley Ross • Marcus Young
• Malina Zlatkova • Michele Perry • Nic Billman
• Rob Hotchkin • Carol Martinez – Compiler

Published by XP Publishing
A department of Christian Services Association
P.O. Box 1017
Maricopa, Arizona 85139
www.XPpublishing.com

ISBN-13: 978-1-936101-34-4

Printed in the United States of America. For worldwide distribution

"Is this not the fast which I choose,
To loosen the bonds of wickedness,
To undo the bands of the yoke,
And to let the oppressed go free
And break every yoke?

"Is it not to divide your bread with the hungry
And bring the homeless poor into the house;
When you see the naked, to cover him;
And not to hide yourself from your own flesh?

"Then your light will break out like the dawn,
And your recovery will speedily spring forth;
And your righteousness will go before you;
The glory of the LORD will be your rear guard.

"Then you will call, and the LORD will answer;
You will cry, and He will say, 'Here I am'
If you remove the yoke from your midst,
The pointing of the finger and speaking wickedness,
And if you give yourself to the hungry
And satisfy the desire of the afflicted,
Then your light will rise in darkness
And your gloom will become like midday.

"And the LORD will continually guide you,
And satisfy your desire in scorched places,
And give strength to your bones;
And you will be like a watered garden,
And like a spring of water whose waters do not fail.

"Those from among you will rebuild the ancient ruins;
You will raise up the age-old foundations;
And you will be called the repairer of the breach,
The restorer of the streets in which to dwell."

Isaiah 58:6-12

TABLE OF CONTENTS

FOREWORD..11
Patricia King

PART ONE – CHILDREN IN CHAINS...............................15

DESCENT INTO TERROR – CHANTEA'S STORY.....................19
Carol Martinez and Malina Zlatkova

LOST AT SEA – NHEAN'S STORY..................................35
Carol Martinez and Malina Zlatkova

RESCUED FROM HATE – CHILD SOLDIERS' STORIES........43
Marcus Young

EXTREME LOVE – A HOPE AND FUTURE REVEALED........53
Malina Zlatkova

PART TWO – IN THE LAND OF THE FREE...............61

RESCUED TO RESCUE OTHERS – SARA'S STORY.............65
Patricia King and Shirley Ross

DIVINE APPOINTMENTS – JOSHUA'S STORY.....................83
Patricia King and Shirley Ross

LOST AND FOUND ON AMERICA'S STREETS – THREE STORIES.......99
Amber Dolson

PART THREE – CHOICES OF DESPERATION..........111

THE TRAGEDY BEHIND A FORCED SMILE –
KOY'S STORY...113
Carol Martinez and Malina Zlatkova

RESCUED FROM SHAME – FON'S STORY.......................125
Carol Martinez and Malina Zlatkova

AMAZING GRACE, THE SPIRITUAL JOURNEY OF A
LADY BOY – MIAOW'S STORY.....................................137
Carol Martinez and Malina Zlatkova

**PART FOUR – LOVE WAR: STORIES FROM
FOOT SOLDIERS ON THE FRONTLINES**............................149

LOVE THAT NEVER FAILS...153
Michele Perry

SHARING THE FATHER'S LOVE ON THE STREETS
OF BRAZIL..167
Nic Billman

THROUGH YOUR PAIN WE KNOW LOVE......................177
Malina Zlatkova

WE JUST HAVE TO KNOW HIM....................................183
Robert Hotchkin

A CALL TO ACTION..197
UNTO THE LEAST OF THESE

PRAY! GIVE! GO!..199
Patricia King

PRAYERS FOR THE CHILDREN...............................201
A COMPILATION OF PRAYERS FOR CHILDREN AT RISK
Patricia King

PRAYER DIRECTIVES.....................................203
FOR SOCIAL JUSTICE MISSIONS

CHRISTIAN MINISTRIES AND ORGANIZATIONS.......205
SERVING IN AREAS OF HUMAN TRAFFICKING, SOCIAL JUSTICE AND MERCY

FOREWORD

I have shed many tears over the last 30 years of ministry – tears of anguish and compassion for those who are suffering, and also tears of joy for the many miracles of healing, deliverance, and redemption I have witnessed in Christ.

The Lord wants us to know His love and compassion for those who are oppressed, for those whose cry is not often heard. He is looking for advocates. He is looking for voices that will represent their needs. He is looking for those who will help fulfill their needs.

The Lord wants us to know His love and compassion for those who are oppressed, for those whose cry is not often heard. He is looking for advocates. He is looking for voices that will represent their needs. He is looking for those who will help fulfill their needs.

I remember walking through the inner city streets of Vancouver years ago, observing the pain in people's eyes. Most of them were addicts and prostitutes, but the pain was very real. At times I would invite one of them for a meal or a coffee and listen to their stories – just listen. All of their stories were horrific; almost all of them had been visited by abuse and neglect from an early age.

A few years later, my husband Ron and I, along with our young boys, spent time living in the inner city of Honolulu. We lived in a rooming house with only one bathroom per floor, which we shared with addicts, thieves, pimps, and prostitutes. Our entire family lived in one room. Rats chewed their way through the screen on our window and made their way in, hiding behind the fridge and under our mattress. Cockroaches ran rampant and we were constantly fighting lice epidemics.

We learned a lot while living amongst the oppressed and the lawless. Again, they all had a story, and most of them were similar – abuse and neglect since childhood. Some of the residents in our building had their own little children whom they abused and neglected. The children were often left alone at night while their moms were "working," and sometimes they were left to fend for themselves all day. We cared for many of those children at the free day care we established in our building after we moved in. Our hearts broke for those little ones. Without intervention, they too would have a story like their parents.

Over the years, we have lived in the slums of Mexico and have visited lawless regions of the Philippines, Thailand, Ghana, Nigeria, Belize, Canada, and the U.S.A. It seems that no matter where you live in the world or what culture you experience, there are those who are trapped in poverty, oppression, addiction, and other forms of bondage. Anywhere in the world you can hear stories of pain. Stories that make you cry.

At this very moment, children are being abducted and trafficked for sex. Little ones are being recruited as soldiers and trained to hate, and murder, for the sake of drug and diamond cartels. And there are children being forced into cruel labor, working long, hard hours for very little.

Multitudes in the world right now have tears bottled up inside that will never be seen by any of us. Many have a hidden cry that will never be heard.

There is One, however, who has seen every tear and heard every cry. There is One who has felt the pain in each of these precious persons. There is One who paid the full price for their freedom. The Lord wants us to be acquainted with these tears and their cries, with the pain and brokenness they represent. He desires compassion to fill us, that we might be compelled to break through for them. Every prayer represents a miracle. Every financial gift represents hope for a better future. Every decision an individual makes to involve themselves with hands-on help represents healing and deliverance for one and for many.

For Their Tears I Died is a book of stories and testimonies that represent tragedy, suffering, and redemption. Some of the stories, although based on true accounts, have been slightly altered to protect the identity and location of the individuals, and also to paint the environment of the accounts with details that will help you engage in the reality of the situations.

For Their Tears I Died is a book that will break your heart with the things that break His. It is a book that will compel you in love and faith to put your hands to the sickle of redemption. You are called to do something... for them... for Him... because, for their tears He died.

And Jesus said,

"Come to the water, stand by My side.

I know you are thirsty, you won't be denied.

I felt every teardrop when in darkness you cried.

And I strove to remind you that for those tears I died."

(Chorus of "For Those Tears I Died." Words and music by Marsha J. and Russ Stevens. © 1972 Communique Music, Inc. Admin. by EMI Christian Music Publishing)

PART ONE:
Children in Chains

The following stories are about the trafficking of minors. These stories are a small representation of a vast crisis that requires immediate, passionate prayer and generous, compassionate action.

There are more slaves today than were seized from Africa in four centuries of the trans-Atlantic slave trade. The modern commerce in humans rivals illegal drug trafficking in its global reach – and in the destruction of lives.

- Approximately 27 million people are enslaved today.

- 80% are women and 50% are children.

- Every minute, two children are trafficked for sexual exploitation.

- The age of the average victim is becoming younger and younger (it is not unusual for 5- and 6-year-olds to be found in brothels).

- Victims are beaten, threatened, drugged, and forced to sleep with upwards of 20 men each day.

- According to INTERPOL, sex trafficking generates $19 billion a year.

"They stole the children, and one of the gang members took a six-year-old kid that I had to look after for three hours. He told me he wanted to see his mommy. Then I started crying and said, 'I don't think you're ever going to see your mommy again.'"

("Maria," a former sex slave kidnapped in Mexico, in an interview given to CNN about how she was forced to look after a little boy about to be sent to the U.S. to satisfy a client's demands.)

"Sympathy is no substitute for action." – *David Livingstone*

CHILDREN IN CHAINS
The Stories

Arise, cry out in the night, as the watches of the night begin;

pour out your heart like water in the presence of the Lord.

Lift up your hands to him for the lives of your children...

Lamentations 2:19 (NIV)

DESCENT INTO TERROR...
Chantea's story

*T*error! You feel suffocated and you try to cry out, but your voice is gone with your breath. Frantic, in your silent scream, you try to move, to run... but you find that your body fails you as your muscles cave under the fear. Maybe you have had a dream like this, and upon waking from the nightmare you expel a huge breath of relief and go get a drink of water, still trying to shake off the clinging tendrils of terror.

Unfortunately, for countless lives all over the world, terror is not a dream out of which they are able to just wake up. They are trapped in the very real terror of sex slavery. They are caught in a powerful web of physical pain, violence, injustice, abuse, sexual degradation, fear, and imprisonment. They live in a world devoid of hope and love, where they are property that is sold to the highest bidder. It is a never-ending, living nightmare that could have only been dreamed up in hell.

Millions of children, some in infancy, live this terror every day of their lives. *This is the story of Chantea.*

§

"Get in!"

Fifteen year-old Chantea stared, confused and terrified, at the man who was pushing her into the trunk of a car. Something was terribly wrong.

Just a few short hours before, this man had appeared at her village hut on the Cambodian-Thai border and introduced himself as a benefactor. He sat with Chantea and her mother in their small hut and sympathized with how hard life could be in the village and their struggle to put food on the table. He expressed concern at the dangers Chantea faced when she crossed illegally into Thailand and worked the fields like so many other girls her age. He voiced outrage that such ones often faced beatings and rape at the hands of Thai soldiers.

Most of the young girls who crossed the borders to work shared and lamented with one another about the abuse and the beatings. But being raped was something none of them ever admitted to. To admit to rape would bring shame and stigma to the victim and dishonor to all of her family. Rape is suffered in silence, but there is whispered gossip when it happens to someone. The man furrowed his brow and shook his head sadly when he said that two girls in Chantea's village had just recently been raped. Then he offered hope...

"I have a solution," the man promised her mother. "I connect good-hearted, wealthy families in Bangkok with young girls from Cambodia who are willing to work as domestic servants in exchange for fair wages and an education. Allow me to take your daughter under this arrangement for a few months. In that short time she will make much more money than she makes in the fields and she will be out of danger. I'll see to it that she sends her monthly wages to you."

Chantea felt something twist inside as the stranger spoke, but he had charmed her mother into trusting him with promises of money and safety. *She didn't want to go with him* – but when her mother said she must, Chantea recognized it as her duty. Fear twisted tighter when the man insisted it was then or never. Chantea glanced at her mother's hopeful face and knew she had no choice.

§

On the Cambodian-Thai border, young girls (and boys) are easy prey to traffickers. There are no jobs, little to eat, and almost all are illiterate. Many of these young children (nine years old or even younger) cross illegally into Thailand several times a week to work in the rice and cane fields. Sometimes they are paid, sometimes they aren't. They are subject to abuse, rape and beatings. Sadly, they are the "lucky" ones. Because when traffickers come into villages in Cambodia, the hills of Thailand, or anywhere else in Southeast Asia, offering "a better life" to the family for the price of one child, almost always the answer is "yes." The offer seems to be a small ray of hope, the only path to survival for the rest of the family. In many cases, the parents literally sell their child, well aware that they will probably end up as sex or labor slaves.

But often, parents (usually single mothers) are deceived into believing that their children are being taken to a better life, where they will work as servants or similar jobs and be given an education. Traffickers often tell them their children will send money home and come back after a time. The traffickers give the parents a small "loan" and the children leave with them, disappearing into the maze of slave traffic. *This is what happened to Chantea.*

§

As they walked away, the man continued to act kindly, smiling and reassuring Chantea that everything would be fine. But as soon as they crossed into Thailand, the charm was gone, replaced by cold disregard. He refused to answer Chantea's questions while they traveled by car to Bangkok. Finally, he sharply told her to shut up. This was nothing new to Chantea. It was how she was usually treated by the people she worked for in the fields – as a non-person, just a working body, not someone with feelings, pain, hopes, and dreams. This was her way of life, but she could never get used to the pain it brought.

After a tense four-hour drive, they reached Bangkok. Stopping at a strange house in a back alley, he allowed Chantea to use the restroom and eat some rice. Then it was time to go. He tightly gripped her thin arm in one hand and said menacingly, "Listen to me carefully. If you make one false move or let out a single sound, you will suffer the consequences severely." She saw he was holding a rope and, realizing what he was about to do with it, Chantea tore her arm from his grasp and bolted toward the door, ready to run as fast as she possibly could. She grabbed the knob and turned it... the door was locked. Immediately he overpowered her, slapping her hard across the face. He roughly bound her hands behind her back and taped her mouth. Then he led her outside, back to the car.

"Get in!" She headed toward the back door of the car, waiting for him to open it up. "No, stupid girl, not there ... here!"

When Chantea balked, he yanked her arm and pushed the petite girl into the trunk. Chantea looked at him - her pleading eyes saying everything her voice would if it could, "Please, sir - I will do what you say, but don't leave me in here. Please, just let me out - anywhere, and I will find my way home. I don't want to go with you anymore. Please... Just let me go home."

He responded with cold, hard eyes. After doing the very same to many other young girls time after time, he well understood the language of pleading, terrified eyes, and wordless whimpers beneath the gagged mouths. But he was not stirred. The small, innocent, totally vulnerable, helpless children like Chantea were nothing but troublesome merchandise to him. Nevertheless, she was worth the hassle; he would be paid well.

Small, innocent, totally vulnerable, helpless children like Chantea were nothing but troublesome merchandise to him.

It was hot and cramped inside the dark trunk. And, oh, so lonely! Terror tightened its hold to the point that even breathing took concentrated effort. It was easier to hold her breath. When she finally did let oxygen in, the smell of diesel caused her to gag. She wanted to throw up and her head throbbed with every movement. Instinctively, she tried to curl up into a protective cocoon, but her arms were tied behind her and she couldn't. The effort only caused the pain in her head and bound arms to intensify.

In the darkness, she touched the small, beaded bracelet on her left wrist, a gift from her mother not too long ago. Hot tears overflowed as she wondered if she would ever see home again.

23

The car moved on for a while – how long, Chantea didn't know – each instant felt like an eternity. Suddenly the vehicle lurched abruptly and her tiny body was thrown against the hard surface inside the trunk. Then she heard muffled voices outside. The moment he opened the trunk, Chantea breathed in deeply, happy for the air. He sat her up for a moment, removed the gag, and put a small cup of water to her lips. "Here, drink this," he commanded. His voice was harsh... but he was offering her water, bringing her hopes up. Maybe, just maybe, he wasn't as cruel as she thought.

Chantea dismissed the bitter taste of the drug-laced water ... it felt good as it poured down her throat, now raw from crying.

What came next happened so quickly she didn't have time to do a double take. For an instant, Chantea saw two frightened faces that mirrored her own – pleading eyes and gagged mouths giving out wordless screams. Then the two young girls were pushed into the trunk, landing on top of Chantea. Sunlight disappeared as the trunk slammed. Three terrified girls – like trapped butterflies with clipped wings – in the dark.

Cramped, with eyes and lungs burning from the suffocating diesel fumes, Chantea thought she would lose her mind as she listened to the two other girls give out their own fearful, gagged gurgles. Mercifully, the drugged water soon took effect and she slipped into welcomed oblivion.

Chantea and the other two girls spent approximately fifteen hours in the trunk, traveling from Bangkok, Thailand, to Kalu Lampur, Malaysia.

Twice the man who'd once seemed so kind woke them up and led them out of the trunk, one at a time, totally disoriented and dazed, into the fields to empty their bladders. He watched them with unflinching eyes as the young girls relieved themselves, even when they, full of shame, begged him to look the other way. Then he took them back to the car, gave them more of the bitter water, and pushed them once again into the trunk where they would submerge into the drugged stupor.

§

"Out! Out now!" Chantea and the other girls woke up to an angry voice in a foreign accent. A strange man was shaking her and pulling her out of the trunk. It was very dark except for the dim car lights. Chantea shook her head, struggling to come out of the fog and back to her senses... where was she? What was she doing here? And then she remembered.

Chantea briefly looked for her supposed "benefactor," but he was nowhere to be seen. She stood in front of two strange men, obviously foreigners, examining her with hard, penetrating eyes and speaking in a language she couldn't understand. Looking up, she saw a third man hauling the other two small, stumbling figures away toward a car in the shadows a short distance away. She realized she was now totally alone. No!!

Drugged, gagged, and terrified, she and the other two girls had never actually spoken to one another during their ordeal. Even so, there had been a silent sisterhood of circumstance between them. And now they had left her behind – with these two strange men.

One of the men wore a large, gem-studded gold ring on his right hand. He said, "Chantea, I paid good money for you. Now you belong to me."

Her mind was still muddled. For some reason, she still thought he simply meant that she would work for him, or for his wife, perhaps. She could begin making money to send back home to

Cambodia. Chantea felt guarded relief. Maybe her ordeal with the cruel man who had tricked her was over, and this man and his wife would treat her well. The twist of fear inside began to ease.

Then the man took Chantea into a house where she met a short, round woman about her mother's age. The woman began to untie Chantea, observing her with small, appraising eyes. Chantea assumed the woman was the man's wife. The woman motioned and in broken Thai said, "Come, follow me." She moved purposefully as she led the young girl down a dim hall.

The woman took Chantea to a bathroom and instructed her to take a shower and put on clothes that had been laid out for her. Chantea had seen these clothes before in magazines and newspapers. These were clothes "bad girls" wore – certainly not her! She looked at the scanty, seductive garments and then, with wide eyes, looked at the woman and shook her head. The woman was unyielding: "Put on! Now! For bed!" Chantea obeyed – she had learned quickly that obeying was important. Then the woman led the freshly scrubbed, tiny Cambodian girl to a small, bare room with a bed.

Chantea was relieved. The bed actually looked good... she was so tired! The arm the man yanked when pulling her out of the trunk was hurting and felt dislocated. The truth was, her whole body ached and she still felt a little dizzy and nauseated from the drugs. But it looked like they were going to allow her to rest a little. She sat on the bed and took a deep breath. Suddenly she heard loud footsteps and men talking. The door to Chantea's room swung open and the owner and two other men filled the small space. Chantea quickly lifted the bed sheet to cover herself. "Leave!" she screamed, "Leave! I am not dressed!"

The owner came over and slapped her violently, causing her nose to gush blood. Forcefully, he ripped the sheet away. He grabbed her and covered her screaming mouth with his large, heavy hand. "Chantea," he said, "I paid good money for you. Now you will work so I can get what I paid for. If you resist, you will just make it harder on yourself. You will get used to it."

In the next instant, all three men were upon her. Terror seized her and would not let go for a very long time. In a few short minutes, Chantea experienced degradation, disgust, horror, and physical pain so intense she felt she would die.

But she didn't die... and thus began a nightmare that went on, and on. Many men raped and beat her day after day. The days turned into weeks, then months. Time lost meaning as she was kept in the small room and used over and over, day and night. Sometimes they chained her to the bed – for punishment, to show who was in control, or for the sheer pleasure of her tormentors. Often she was beaten for no other reason than the perverted compulsion of the clients. Yet despite her cracked ribs, black eyes, bruised face and damaged heart, there was always another client demanding his pleasure.

Chantea was not alone. She was imprisoned in a brothel with a couple dozen other young girls, all in bondage to serve the depraved appetites of the constant trail of men.

The "mamasan," the woman she met when she first arrived, and the boss, usually kept Chantea drugged so she would be more compliant. The drugs made her weak and groggy, but did nothing to numb the pain and suffocating shame. She was unable to resist or flee. Chantea realized that if she did get out, she had no idea where to go or what to do.

She lived, confined in despair. No longer knowing if it was night or day, she wondered if she would ever freely walk outside, feel sunlight on her face, or breathe the fresh air again. She could no longer remember how it felt to not have the hard knot of fear twist in her stomach. She felt alone, abandoned, and forgotten. Her world had been reduced to rough grasping hands, stale breath, harsh words, sexual abuse, and fists. Tenderness and comfort were from another life, wisps of mist in her memory. As she would touch the worn beads on her wrist that she had somehow managed to keep, she wondered if her mother ever thought of her.

Unknown to Chantea, her mother had not forgotten her. She had believed the trafficker when he promised he would return with news and money from her daughter. After several months of silence, she became very concerned. A social worker from a Christian ministry involved in rescuing and restoring trafficked children visited Chantea's village one day and met her mother, who shared her story and concerns, giving them a picture of Chantea and other vital information.

Divine intervention, along with wise networking by the ministry leader, produced an incredible breakthrough. When they showed Chantea's picture in the Bangkok red light district, a woman actually recognized her! She had also been trafficked into Malaysia and forced into prostitution in the very brothel Chantea was trapped in. This type of life ages the women very quickly, so after some time the pimps had decided she was too old and unattractive and they let her go. Thanks to her tip, experts in this kind of rescue went to Malaysia on a mission to search specifically for little Chantea.

§

Chantea had been in captivity for over a year when she overheard the mamasan and pimps talking about her in hushed tones outside her room. The door opened and her "owner" came in, ordering her to leave with him. For reasons unknown to Chantea, they sent her into hiding for several days.

The flight was caused by two people who had come undercover trying to find her and get her released. As soon as the pimps thought it was safe again, Chantea was returned to the brothel and life went back to normal.

But one day, not too long after...

"Chantea! Come now!" It was the mamasan calling her. There were two men waiting. "New men!" she added. Chantea braced herself. She still felt sick every time she had to go into one of the rooms. She still feared it and hated it. When she knew there would be more than one man, all those feelings were intensified. She never knew what exactly was going to happen to her, she just knew it was never good. She was just 16, but she was very old!

When she entered the room, Chantea was surprised that the men were still fully dressed. She was about to say something when one of them covered her mouth. Oh, no! What did this mean? But his hand was gentle. The other man did not smile; he just stood taut, like a trap ready to spring. However, there was something in his expression that was very different from what she had seen in others. "Chantea," he said, "we are here to help you. You must trust us and do as we say. You are about to be free!"

Rescue? Chantea's heart leaped with hope, but fell hard as fear's familiar hand constricted, taking her breath away. The rush of excitement quickly evaporated and distrust set in. What kind of game was this? What did these men want? What were they going to do to her? That someone could be good just for the sake of being good was no longer in her set of beliefs.

Large sums of money were paid to set things in motion to free Chantea. But she was worth it!

After investigating a number of brothels, they had finally been able to locate Chantea. The brothel operator first denied she was there and hid her, but through a sting operation they finally got through. Large sums of money were paid to set things in motion to free her. But Chantea was worth it! So very worth it!

§

The people who rescued her returned her to Cambodia. She was brought to a home where kindness welcomed her. Misty memories of tenderness and warmth began to take on substance as Chantea was cleaned up and fed good food by people who listened and comforted her. She stayed on guard, believing there had to be an ulterior motive. She had trusted before, with disastrous results. They took her to the doctor and nursed her broken body, nurturing her to better health. But Chantea's soul was still broken. She continued to wait for whatever would be demanded of her. This kindness could not be free.

One day one of the workers came with news. "Chantea, we have been talking with your mom and she is eager to see you! She doesn't want you to go to your village because she doesn't want you to feel shame. So we are making arrangements for the two of you to move to another village together."

Chantea looked into the compassionate eyes of the woman before her. She looked for the lie, but could not find it. It was true! She was about to see her mother again! Suddenly the knot of fear released and hope rushed in. The workers reassured her that the only reason they had known about her and had searched for her was because of her mother.

Chantea found it hard to believe, still guarding her heart from another betrayal. Now they were saying she would soon see her mother and receive a home and provision so they could live together in another village where no one knew her. For the first time in many months, Chantea looked at her mother's gift – the wired beads around her wrist – with joy instead of despair.

Chantea was overwhelmed with feelings she had not felt in a long time, feelings the young girl had forgotten existed. She barely heard the woman say that they were also sending her to their sewing school where she would learn how to become a seamstress. She would have an honest and dignified means to support herself and her mother.

Who were these people anyway? Why were they so kind to her? Why did they care and do so much, expecting nothing in return? Not even the spirit gods had cared for her – and yet these people did!

She knew it was time to find out why. She had asked before, but had not been able to believe their words about Jesus as true. When she asked, they smiled and spoke again of Jesus' love for her. "Chantea," they said, "You did not have a choice when it happened, when evil men exchanged money in order to place you in the terrible bondage you suffered. Then we paid a price in order to set you free from the brothel, and you were so worth it! But nothing compares with the price Jesus paid for you. You are so greatly valued by God Himself that Jesus, His only Son, was willing to suffer cruel injustice on your behalf and pay the price of your redemption with His blood on the cross. He loves you so much!"

This time, when they told her, she believed! How could she not? She embraced His love, and has delighted in His embrace ever since! Her road to full recovery has not been short and easy, but every day she wakes up to her loving Father's tender new mercies with the same trust and hope a child places in their loving father. Now, not only is her body free, but so is her heart and soul!

> Chantea's road to full recovery has not been short and easy, but every day she wakes up to her loving Father's tender new mercies with trust and hope.

The people in the village where she lives now do not know her whole story. Out of respect for her mother she has kept quiet, since it is such a stigma. But the villagers are drawn to the young seamstress with the soft smile and voice. They are very impressed with her work ethic and excellence. When someone comments that there is something special and different about her, she immediately answers, "It's because I love and serve a very special God! It is His love and care that makes me this way." And they listen.

Chantea was *never* forgotten! God knew about her and loved her all along. He knew the terrible pain she suffered, and He knew the tears she shed. All of heaven rejoiced when she was finally set free. Freedom from her captors and freedom through knowing and embracing the Father, because, *for her tears, yes, her tears, Jesus died.*

This story is based on a true account of a young woman girl rescued and helped by Cambodian Hope Organization, as told to Carol Martinez and Malina Zlatkova. Names have been changed as well as some of the details. For more information about Cambodian Hope Organization and to learn how you can become involved, visit cambodianhopeorganization.org.

I will contend with those who contend with you,

and your children I will save.

Isaiah 49:25 (NIV)

LOST AT SEA
Nhean's Story

*T*he news wasn't good for Kunthea, a single mother of three in a small jungle village near the Thai-Cambodian border. The doctor at the public hospital told her she had a serious illness, and her only hope of getting better depended on her taking the expensive medicine he had prescribed for her.

But how? The hospital couldn't provide the medicine and she didn't have the means to purchase it. She was too sick to work and didn't have money to support her children, let alone buy medicine! She was quickly running out of the little food she had to feed them and wondered how they would survive once she died. What could she do? She was desperate and alone – oh, so alone!

The day the strange man came to visit her was what she thought was an answer to her prayers to the gods. He seemed genuinely kind and concerned as he said, "I've heard how sick you are and that you need money to get well. Let me help. I have connections and can get your oldest son a good job in Thailand. I'll arrange for him to send you money monthly. To prove to you my good faith, I will give you 250,000 riel in advance money."

When she heard the amount, she was immediately excited. This seemed too good to be true! Even though it is the equivalent of about 50 U.S. dollars, it was an enormous sum to Kunthea. With that amount of money she could purchase the medicine she needed to help her get well, as well as provide food for her other two children. And now there was the promise of regular income!

Thirteen-year-old Nhean felt differently, though. The thought of leaving his mother and younger siblings and going off with this strange man terrified him. But he didn't have a choice. Either he worked to support his family or his mother would die, leaving him and his two younger brothers alone to fend for themselves. And then he would be shunned for having dishonored his family.

"Don't worry, son," his mother reassured him, "it will all turn out well. After you make enough money you can come back to us." Even so, his mind felt clouded and dazed. His last memory was of his two little brothers crying as they watched him walk away with the strange man.

§

Mr. Wattana smuggled Nhean into Aranyupeth, a Thai border town. Nhean was told that they would be going to a city where he would be put to work in a restaurant or something similar. But now Mr. Wattana gave him some unexpected news: "I've found a great job for you on a fishing boat. Don't worry, you will be well taken care of. Even though you will work hard some days, on other days they will let you rest. You will come back to shore almost every day." The thought of being out in the ocean frightened Nhean, but Mr. Wattana's reassuring words helped a little. When he led Nhean to the fishing boat, everyone there seemed very occupied and didn't say much to him. That first evening he was fed a decent meal, so he felt a little more peace.

Neither he nor his mother knew that they had been deceived. But the truth was that Mr. Wattana was a trafficking agent who had just sold him to the captain of a fishing trawler. Every year, tens of thousands of boys and young men - mostly Cambodian - are tricked or literally kidnapped off the streets and trafficked, forced to work on these fishing boats for months on end without returning to land. Many never return.

Every year, tens of thousands of boys and young men are trafficked, forced to work on fishing boats for months on end. Many never return.

After Nhean and some other young boys got on the boat, it went deep into the ocean and did not return to shore the next day as Mr. Wattana had promised. Nor the next. Instead, every day the trawler went further and further into sea, and Nhean's nightmare began. He, along with the other trafficked workers, was forced to work day and night, sleeping only two or three hours. Some days he wasn't allowed to sleep at all, working to the sounds of yells and threats. When the men in charge determined he wasn't being productive enough, he was beaten severely. And there was always the threat of more beatings.

Obviously, his strength soon gave out, but then they would give him "sweet water." This drug-laced beverage gave him an exhilarating feeling, making him feel stronger than he actually was and enabling him to work willingly. But it also clouded his thoughts, making him confused and dazed. The long hours in the sun and diet of nothing but fish, combined with the ever-increasing drugs, severely deteriorated his mental and physical condition.

He lived in constant fear. He heard stories of crew members actually being thrown off the boat into the deep sea, or being beaten with heavy hooks and equipment. He knew the beatings were particularly severe if someone tried to escape. But in the middle of the sea there was nowhere to go unless you chose to leap into the water and drown. It was almost understandable why some preferred that to the slow death they experienced on the boat. Many didn't survive the harsh conditions. They became seriously ill, emaciated, emotionally disturbed, and unable to see, hear, or walk properly. Sometimes, those who were too sick to continue working were cast into the waters.

They had been at sea for six months when one day they approached land. Though Nhean's body was frail and weakened and his mind muddled, the instinct for survival strengthened him. So when he saw an opportunity to escape, he jumped ship and began to run. He didn't get very far, though. The police spotted him immediately and there was no way he could outrun them.

They began to question him, but his mind was so deteriorated, he wasn't able to answer any of their questions. He wasn't even able to tell them where he was from. So they treated the confused, sick, and emaciated thirteen-year-old as they treated most illegal aliens, no matter what age. They threw him in jail with little water or food and no medical care whatsoever.

But Nhean was far from forgotten. Back in his village in Cambodia, his mother, who was now enjoying better health, was very concerned about her son. The man who had promised her so much when he took her son had not returned to the village, and she hadn't heard news from him or her Nhean. Where was he? She sensed that something terrible had happened to her son, but she would not give up hope that he could be found. Then one day, staff members of CHO, Cambodian Hope Organization, went to Nhean's home village. When his mother found out that they could possibly help, she immediately went to them and told them her story. She also provided them with a picture.

The staff of CHO immediately went to work. They work closely with both Cambodian and Thai authorities because they recognize this is the best way to do things. They sent a picture of Nhean to Thai officials and asked them to please find him. Miraculously, they were able to locate him. CHO spent two weeks doing the necessary paperwork and put out all the necessary funds to get Nhean out of the Thai jail and transported back to Cambodia.

§

Kunthea was startled when she saw her son for the first time after his return. Was it really her Nhean? He was totally skin and bones and looked very old – like an old man. He was also severely mentally damaged. Very little of the Nhean she once knew was there. Her heart broke. She would never let him go again!

CHO has a special program to help trafficked children recuperate. When children at such a young age go through such horrifying experiences, it can take a long time for them to get better. They are totally disoriented. Many, like Nhean, can't even remember where they are from or who their family is. Others are scared and want to kill themselves. They are very aggressive with others, always ready to fight. Those who have been on drugs have to go through the withdrawal process. To complicate matters, understandably they are full of fear and mistrust, so one of the first hurdles the staff encounters is winning the children's trust so they can actually help them. Pastors, counselors, social workers, and medical personnel combine their areas of expertise with God's patient and unconditional love and prayer – lots of prayer – and are there around the clock bringing these children to full restoration.

> Usually, it takes rescued children a long time to get better. Pastors, counselors, and medical personnel combine their expertise with God's love and lots of prayer, working around the clock to bring them to full restoration.

Kunthea wasn't ready to release her son into the program at first. So CHO even went the extra mile. They provided her with the means to start a micro-enterprise to support herself, her family and, at the same time, stay close to her long-lost son while they cared for him. Nhean did get better. On his road to recovery, he learned that there was Someone who would always be worthy of his trust; he and all of his family embraced this loving God. Once he was better, he spent a year under CHO's vocational training program and learned how to repair motorcycles.

Nhean is still a teen-ager, but now, he and his family are back in their home village where he has a motorcycle repair business.

Motorcycles are Cambodia's chief means of transportation, so he keeps busy, and there is always food on the table. God is so good!

There is, however, a deep concern in Nhean's heart that never lets go. He shares, "There are many young boys just like me who are suffering the same things I did, or are in danger of being sold like I was. Can you please help them?"

Nhean's story reminds us one more time that no one is ever lost to God. In whatever corner of the earth, God sees them. No matter what harsh conditions, terrible injustice and pain they are going through, God sees it. And though they are the suffering victims of cruel, vile hatred, God passionately loves them. ***It is for their tears that Jesus died.***

God's heart breaks for all the "Nheans" who suffer this kind of slavery on high waters just so others may have cheap fish on their plate.

Can you see Nhean? Close your eyes for a moment... imagine this young man then – and now. Imagine what it would be like if the tens of thousands of young boys who have endured what he has endured could have the same happy ending.

Perhaps they can. Perhaps they can.

This story is based on a true account of a young boy rescued and helped by Cambodian Hope Organization, as told to Carol Martinez and Malina Zlatkova. Names and some of the details have been slightly changed. For more information about Cambodian Hope Organization and to learn how you can become involved, visit cambodianhopeorganization.org.

For he does not willingly bring affliction or
grief to the children of men.

Lamentations 3:33 (NIV)

Rescued from Hate
Child soldiers' stories

Abandoned to the Army

When I was six, my parents gave me to the army. Early in the morning my father pulled me out of sleep. It was still dark. He packed me on his back down the mountain trail from the village. His long black hair tickled my nose all the way. After we came to the main road I had to walk. We walked most of the day. I had no water and my throat was chalky dry because it was the time of no rain. We walked between the rocks in the red powder of the earth as the red sun beat upon my head.

Finally we came to a cluster of houses. At the side of the road was a tin roofed lean-to. Men with guns sat in the shade of the slanted roof while others stood in the shadow of a great tree that

43

spread its frog-like limb's over the road. They looked mean and I was scared, but my father walked over to them. He left me near the base of the tree and went to talk with some of the men near a truck. I played with a dung beetle in the dirt.

My parents disowned me. I don't know why. Maybe there was not enough food and my older brothers could help Father better than I could.

Finally father turned away from the men and began walking down the road. He never even looked at me. I thought he had forgotten me. I cried out, "Papa," but he did not turn back. I began to run after him but one of the men in green caught me by the arm and cuffed me. "You stay here," he slurred at me. I was shocked. I tried to lunge away but he struck me again.

That evening they threw me on top of the supplies that awkwardly filled the truck, and they told me to hold on or die. We drove all night till my arms ached and my skin stung sore from the dust and wind. In the morning we arrived at a town and drove up to a cement and metal fence. This was to be my prison. I did not know what a prison was. I did not even know what an army was. But now I know because I have lived in this place of no escape. I later found out my parents had offered me for nothing, I was not even worth a few coins!

Some of my friends came here because they were orphans. Some of them were conscripted. Others were abandoned. I was one of the most unfortunate – or so I thought. My parents disowned me. I don't know why. Maybe, as I learn more about my world... I think there was not enough food and my mother's stomach was taut with a coming child. Another still nursed at her breast. My two brothers, both older than me, worked hard on the farm. They could help Father better than I could – I heard them say it.

Lessons from the Rope

My first morning, I still remember. I woke that day to the rhythm of the rope upon my body. The song of the rope I know well now. It woke us very early every morning, before the great light had risen in the sky. It struck the flesh of all who were not rising from sleep quickly enough. Most of us did not wake unless we had to. Our bodies ached fearfully, and in sleep we could forget... The rope that bit our flesh seldom causes us to bleed, but there were times... oh, yes... there were times.

We would gather to attention in the courtyard. There we stood and drilled. Every day was the same. The rope was our companion as we marched out to the fields to work. All of us had to labor in the fields. We also worked in rock quarries, we built roads, we carried the burdens of the soldiers – sometimes many days – on foot. If we had ridden on a truck to work, we would have been like pigs going to market. And who would want to do that? We would be going to market just to be slaughtered. Yes, we learned that we were animals – the difference was, we could speak while other beasts are dumb.

After a stretch of work in the morning, we would get a break. We were given food in dirty, cracked bowls: rice with some vegetable broth. It gurgled painfully into the knot that lived and twisted in my stomach. I think it was an angry spirit that came to steal what little food I got. At night I was given maybe half a bowl of the same food ... if I was fortunate. If we tried to take more, the rope slithered across our shoulders. The rope's only comfort was that it was familiar.

Training for Soldiering

The year I was numbered eight years old, they began to teach me to be tough, to hate, to have a heart to kill my enemies. This was easy. My only family was the army, and I hated them, too. I couldn't run away, though, as there was nowhere to hide. A few years before, many of my friends ran away. I thought I heard the guns barking in the distance, but I don't know. Only a few returned out of the many children that fled.

> They began to teach me to be tough, to hate, to have a heart to kill my enemies. This was easy. My only family was the army and I hated them, too.

Near my tenth year, I began to train with weapons when my instructors decided it was time. This was good because I spent less time quarrying rock so my back and legs did not ache as much. Because so many of my friends died, there is still a void in my heart. Some of my other friends would go and bed down with the older soldiers at night. They escaped the sound of the rope in the morning. Afterwards there was money in their pockets to buy small things, but I felt scared because many of them wept in the days that followed. Some became very sick and if we are sick in that place we most likely die. There is no help and no hope for the sick there. The spirits were very powerful.

What is death like? Do I wander around like a ghost or can I just forget that I am alive and sleep a very deep sleep? These are the questions I questioned myself with sometimes, but most days were too difficult for the lips of my thoughts to speak to me.

The Rescue

I was nearly twelve when it happened. It was almost my time to begin as one of those who were entrusted with guns. I thought maybe it had something to do with that. The soldiers lined us up and began to sort through our ranks. I saw they were choosing the worst of us, the weakest. I was chosen because I had a limp from a falling rock in the quarry. I tried to stand straight so I would not be hit but my shirt was too tight. Some years my clothes hung loose, some years they fit almost right. That day my clothes pinched my shoulders. I only had the clothes that were on my back. They were going to give me a real soldier's outfit when I turned twelve.

A man with a smile walked around us and took pictures. He put his hand on my shoulder. I shuddered. I still remembered my friends. Most of them had painful sickness that people say came from laying near the soldiers. I didn't like it when men smiled at me. But now we were told we had been cast off from the army and this man was taking us because we were no good anymore.

Several moon cycles later I was still in the army.[1] I wondered some days what would happen when I left. The army was almost my only memory. Then I became very sick. My mind wandered and I cried for my father to come back and take me home. That day I could not get up when the rope beat its tattoo on my side. Later they piled my hot body into a truck. I lay among the others while we were driven to the place I now live. I think we were all very sick.

Then we arrived at this new place I now call home. It was like a dream ... children came out of that place and helped me down.

[1]Editor's note: Even though the rescue process had begun, it still took some time before he and the others were finally released and taken to a home.

They looked very fat so I was sure I was dreaming. At first we shared the beds of these nice, fat children because there was no place for us. Their beds were very soft. The other children were kind and so were the adults. I did not see any soldiers. Every day they fed us rice porridge and gave us medicine. I was told this was my new home.

> They told me about a Father who lives in Heaven who sent His son Jesus to look for me and when He found me He brought me here, to this place, just because He loves me.

They told me about a Father who lives in heaven who sent His Son Jesus to look for me and when He found me He brought me here, to this place, just because He loves me so much. At first I could not believe, but then I did not die when I knew I should have. And the people were so kind. I had three meals a day and warm blankets, a change of clothes and new shoes. I even used soap for the first time in my life. I wept many tears that first night when I was in my bed.

Now I have been here one year. At night we all gather to sing songs of thanks to this Father in heaven and His Son who came to be with us. We feel Him so near us when we sing and pray. I have decided that I will follow this Jesus. He is also a soldier, I am told, but He is strong because He is love. I do not understand all this but I know that I have been rescued and it is God in heaven that I want to follow.

Sanan's Story

Hi, my name is Sanan. I'm now about 14 years old and my heart is so full of gratefulness because Divine Inheritance called for me to come live at their children's home. I feel very safe here. I also hope for my future. When I was a soldier, I had no hope at all, no dream for life. This is the story of my hardship.

My father lived as a soldier and my mother died when I was six months old, so I grew up around the army. One terrible day, news arrived about my father. He was made a prisoner of war by the national army that our people fought and resisted for the sake of freedom. I was seven years old the day the messenger came from the war front ... it still burns like a hot rock in my memory.

After that day, some relatives came to get me so that I would have a future. But my relatives treated me shamefully and without honesty. When I was nine, the army came to conscript from their family, but my relatives sent me instead of their own children. I did not want to be a soldier. I hated soldiering because I had lost my father in a battle. War had already ruined my life, and the army was the last place I wanted to be.

I served in the army for three years of agony. My first day, the "boss" soldier boy had me gang raped. Then they sent me out to collect old bottles and cans to sell for recycle. I had to pay my dues to the boy soldier leaders. Most of the time, I never could sell what I found and I was all the time in their debt. I was so stressed because I couldn't pay so that they had money to spend. Every day, they would torture me, especially when I couldn't do what they

> I served in the army for three years of agony. My first day, the "boss" soldier boy had me gang raped. Then he sent me out to collect old bottles and cans to sell for recycle.

49

commanded me. I was their personal slave whenever I was free from my soldier duties.

When I was soldiering, I had 24-hour sentry watches and was forced to keep alert during very hot days and cold windy mountain nights. I scoured the hillsides many miles for firewood, split the wood, and worked the farms. Early mornings were military trainings and long runs. At night, I would lie awake and cry.

I used to be scared of dark spirits in the hills and trees, but now I get to experience God's love toward me and God's hope for me.

I had no blanket for comfort, even when it was cold and the wind blew through the bamboo barracks. I lay there alone with my tears and my longing that father would escape and come rescue me from my misery.

But now that I have been rescued, my house parents are kind and urge me to be diligent. They are good to me, like my own parents would have been. They guide me on the path to my goal. I used to be scared of dark spirits in the hills and trees, but now I get to experience Jesus' love toward me and God's hope for me. I want to serve God and tell many people about His Jesus. So please help me and pray for me, that one day I can help my people, like you have helped me.

The first story is a compilation of the lives of different children rescued by Divine Inheritance, led by Marcus Young. Circumstances, details and events have been mixed. This protects the children's lives and identities. However, this compilation is based on real stories and is an accurate representation of the life of a child in the armies that use children in Southeast Asia. The second story is from a single account.

It is not the will of your Father who is in heaven
that one of these little ones perish.

Matthew 18:14

EXTREME LOVE
A Hope and Future Revealed

We have a beautiful picture of Jesus from the New Testament gathering children to Himself, laughing with them, enjoying and loving and blessing each and every one. It is a scene of safety and joy, each child precious to Him. He rebuked anyone who would keep a child from Him.

God sees each child as precious, with a wealth of destiny inside them. He loves their unfailing trust, guileless hearts, freedom, and inquisitive nature. We love to see children smiling, laughing, playing, dancing, and singing.

But unfortunately a much darker picture emerges as we see the statistics citing over a million children every year forced into a very different life, a life that was never intended for them, and one that breaks the heart of Father God. Such was the life of Jorani, a little jewel found in the trash heap.

§

When eight-year-old Jorani was found early one morning in a garbage dump in the back streets of a Thai city, flies were already covering her. She was unconscious and barely breathing; it was a miracle she was alive. The tiny, frail body – more like that of a four- or five-year-old – was hot to the touch, ravaged with fever. Her matchstick thin arms and legs were full of needle marks and bruises; her big round eyes, sunken into dark, deep sockets. Her hair was reddish instead of black, her skin tone patchy and pasty – other indications of extreme malnutrition. The back of the filthy, tattered pants she had on was soaked in blood. This was just Jorani's external appearance. The laborer who found her was moved with compassion. He picked her up and rushed her to the emergency room of the closest public hospital. Given her condition – and what was behind it – some debated whether perhaps it would have been more merciful to have simply left her there to die.

Her outward appearance was hard to take in, but the outcome of the doctor's examination was much more troubling. X-rays showed evidence of fractures on almost every bone in her body – her legs, arms, ribs, and even her cheekbones. Lab tests showed that her fever was both from an STD (sexually transmitted disease) and a urinary tract infection. Both the visual and internal examination the doctor performed on her "private parts" and reproductive organs showed evidence that her vagina had been torn and sewn up again at least a couple of times. Her internal organs were totally out of alignment. Without reconstructive surgery, it was highly unlikely she would ever again be able to normally perform the bodily functions most of us take for granted.

Sadly, this was not the first time the medical personnel had seen a case like this. They would clean her up, feed her, and take care of her most immediate needs. But after that, what would happen to her? Where would she go? What kind of life could she expect?

Exactly who was this little girl? And how did she end up in the garbage dump?

§

Jorani is actually a composite of hundreds of young children – boys, girls, and sometimes babies – who are forced into sex slavery. She or he may have come from Cambodia, Myanmar, Laos, Vietnam, or the hill country of Thailand. They may have been abandoned orphans, or kidnapped by traffickers, or sold by their own families. Sometimes, the parents are fooled into thinking the child will be offered a better life in the city as a house servant or something similar. Sadly, many times the parents know exactly what the child will end up being forced to do. But they feel they have no other choice – either one child is sacrificed for a price, or the entire family is at risk of starvation. It is hard to believe that $50 to $100 given in exchange for a son or daughter would make such a difference in an entire family's life, but such is the case in desperate times.

We have given this little girl the name Jorani because it means "radiant jewel" in Khmer (Cambodian language), a reminder of God's desire and intended destiny for all little boys and girls. But her life, and the lives of the hundreds of thousands of children who are forced into sexual slavery each year, is worse than that of an abused dog eventually rescued by an animal welfare organization. Once these little boys and girls reach their target cities in Thailand, they are imprisoned in brothels in back alleys, under lock and chain – sometimes not just to a room or building, but to a bed. We heard a case of a four-year-old little girl chained to a bed for two years. Imagine! For two years all she saw was the ceiling and "clients."

> Once these little boys and girls reach their target cities, they are imprisoned in brothels in back alleys, under lock and chain — sometimes not just to a room or building, but to a bed.

These little boys and girls are repeatedly raped, day after day, hour after hour, by pedophiles who come from all over the world solely for this purpose. We have gone into pedophile areas of the city and see westerners there, with little boys on their knees. It is sickening because we know what is going to happen next. One little boy we were able to help had dirt caked under his fingernails. He had dug his fingers into the ground as he was "taken" in the back alley streets.

They are subject to gang rapes and every kind of torture imaginable. They are drugged day in and day out, removing all resistance from them. Because virgins can be sold out at a very high price, little girls are often sewn up, without anesthesia, and sold again as "virgins." Since little boys still aren't developed enough to perform, male animal hormones are often injected into them. This causes terrible reactions and often they die, unable to bear it.

As in the case of our composite child, Jorani, they are typically used and then discarded when they become too ill or disabled to make money for their abusers. So what happens to them then?

The Thai government has a system for identifying pedophile brothels and arresting the perpetrators. The local police in partnership with an organization called Fight Against Child Exploitation (FACE) identify suspected brothels in the area surrounding Bangkok and Pattaya. When they have sufficient information, they perform a raid. The Thai children found in the brothel are placed in a short-term safe house where they remain for one to four months. They receive medical care, safe housing, and some counseling.

Unfortunately, at least half the children found in the brothels are not Thai. Some are tribal children who have no rights to education, medical care, or to be in a Thai shelter. If the children are from Laos, Cambodia, Vietnam, or Myanmar, they are placed in adult refugee shelters. Though they are innocent pawns, the children continue to be victimized with rape and abuse in these settings. No medical care is provided, except in emergency, and there is no emotional care. They are kept until their immigration papers are found. If no papers are found, the children are typically dumped at the border of their home country with no money or support. They then become vulnerable to continued maltreatment and are placed back into situations where they will once again fall prey to traffickers.

Thus, even when a child can be identified and extricated from a brothel or other enslaved situation, their problems do not end there. Though there are organizations, such as FACE, working on identifying the perpetrators, few programs have been developed to address the healing and re-humanization of the children.

Thanks to the prayers and offerings of many caring people, a number of Christian shelters for trafficked children are being set up. Without centers like these, Jorani's future, if she were to survive, would be at risk. But thankfully, Jorani was referred to such a home by the Thai authorities. The following could very well be the story of countless other children. One by one, the Home accepts a broken child and begins the mending process as they make real the heart of God, bringing light into darkness.

When Jorani arrived, she was still very ill, very frightened and traumatized. It is said that a child's emotional development is stunted at the age when she is first raped. She showed no emotions and did not respond in any way to the loving, patient care of those at the home. Caring medical personnel looked after her medical needs, even planning for reconstructive surgery once she was stronger – both physically and emotionally. As her physical body healed, the staff worked to bring healing to her soul. Eventually, she relaxed a little, but still stayed very guarded. She would have outbursts of rage and at other times be very withdrawn. The house parents were patient, giving love, support, and comfort freely. Jorani would wake up at night with nightmares, and sometimes she would have trouble breathing as she remembered the trauma. Often the house parents would just sit with her in a rocking chair and rock her.

During the day, Jorani and the other children were given art projects or toys and taught to play again. Slowly life returned to her eyes, as her heart felt safe and began to heal. The Home also worked to get Jorani the papers she needed in order either to return home or be placed in a long-term Christian facility in her own country that would care for her and teach her a trade. One life saved out of so many in need.

God sees every one of these precious children that are treated as garbage, and He weeps over them. Will you help? Will you be a part of taking these discarded jewels and restoring to them the radiance God intended for them? **It is for their tears that Jesus died!**

This chapter is by Malina Zlatkova, XPMissions' representative in Southeast Asia. Her passion for children and their wellbeing has resulted in the development of projects that aim to save and heal trafficked children in the region. In 2010, the Extreme Love Children's Home was established. For more information and to learn how you can become involved, vist xpmissions.com.

PART TWO:
In the Land of the Free

We hear about the horrors of sex trafficking in Southeast Asia and other places far away, but the shocking truth is that children and young men and women are subject to the same kinds of abuse in our own backyard. Some are trafficked in from other countries – often drugged, then hidden in shipping containers like merchandise. Others are U.S. citizens – runaways, homeless, or kidnapped from their families. The following stories are accounts from the United States and Canada.

SEX TRAFFICKING OF CHILDREN IN THE UNITED STATES

- Each year, at least 100,000 children are victimized through prostitution within the U.S.

- The average age of entry into prostitution in the United States is 13 years old.

- Many organized crime and gang rings have turned to selling children/teens rather than drugs and guns.

- Sex trafficking is very lucrative and difficult to prosecute.

- Children exploited through prostitution suffer post-traumatic stress and other mental health issues, physical health problems including STDs, and substance addictions.

- There are reports that there are fewer than 100 beds nationwide in shelters prepared to provide the specialized care exploited children need.

- The State Department's 2010 Trafficking in Persons Report included the recommendation for the U.S. to increase "efforts to identify and assist U.S. citizen victims" and "increase funding for victims' services."

- Sex trafficking of minors happens in every state, to children of every ethnic and economic background.

"For weeks, Jessica's captors kept her hostage in an apartment in one of Phoenix's most dangerous neighborhoods. After days of physical and mental abuse, they forced her to dress up, then took a picture of her and placed her on craigslist. Shortly after the ad posted, men began to arrive. Each of them pleasured themselves at the expense of Jessica's innocence." (*Jessica's story – Unchained Generation*)

How shall I feel at the judgment, if multitudes of missed opportunities pass before me in full review, and all my excuses prove to be disguises of my cowardice and pride? *–W. E. Sangster*

IN THE LAND OF THE FREE
The Stories

The Spirit of the Lord GOD is upon me,

Because the LORD has anointed me

To bring good news to the afflicted;

He has sent me to bind up the brokenhearted,

To proclaim liberty to captives

And freedom to prisoners...

Isaiah 61:1

RESCUED TO RESCUE OTHERS

Sara's Story

*H*ow does a young girl raised in an upper middle-class American neighborhood become a drug-addicted prostitute at the age of 13? This is Sara's account.

I was raised in an upper middle-class neighborhood in a prestigious house with a perfectly manicured lawn and highline cars parked in the garage. With a well-dressed, successful father and a mother who attended church every Sunday, my family was considered to be a pillar of society – on the outside. On the inside, however, no one knew about the monster that prowled the halls at night taking hushed, yet violent, liberties in his five-year-old daughter's bedroom.

Something fractures the mind and soul of a little girl when her daddy molests her. It's the ultimate betrayal – when a father secretly abuses his little girl to fulfill his own rants and pleasures, strips her of self-worth, and sends her into the world without a shred of covering. The chances of her survival are very slim.

When I turned eight, my father's violence against my mother escalated out of control, leaving her one day with a fractured skull on our living room floor. I stood there in terror as the beating took place in my presence. My father had to have everything in its place – everything had to be perfect. And if it wasn't, his violence would manifest. I was frozen as I looked at my mom unconscious on the floor. My first thought was how we would ever get all that blood off the carpet before "the monster" returned. I sat next to my mom for hours, listening to her breath become more and more faint. I knew she was dying, but I was too afraid to call for help. I'd been thoroughly warned about what would happen if anyone ever found out what was happening inside the "perfect house." Fear of the monster's rage had taught me to lie really well. While I laid beside my dying mom, all I could think about were ways to explain away the truth to protect his flawless reputation.

> Something fractures the mind and soul of a little girl when her daddy molests her to fulfill his own rants and pleasures.
>
> It is the ultimate betrayal.

It is all a blur to me now as to when and how the authorities found us, but I do remember the police, paramedics, and other emergency personnel storming into the room. I remember being frozen in fear, but I don't remember much else.

Abandoned to the System

My mother died, my father went to prison, and I ended up in a foster home. I was branded as the girl with emotional problems whose father killed her mother. The "emotional problems" always puzzled me, because I didn't have emotions like my foster brother and sister did. They were very disturbed and I was quiet. So why did they say I had the problem? At first no one knew what to say to me – so they just left me alone, which was fine with me.

Then the light under the bedroom door that I watched so closely each night began to darken. Seth, the thirteen-year-old son of my foster parents, had developed a curiosity about my mother's death and began making secret visits to my room at night to "talk." He had me tell him the story over and over, each time asking more questions to help him paint a more vivid picture in his twisted imagination. Because his satisfaction and approval, no matter how morbid, were the only things that mattered (or at least that's what I had been taught), I found myself adding details that weren't even true.

His excitement during our story time turned sexual one night. What happened wasn't new to me, but it soon turned him into a little monster. The secret "night visits" continued for over a year, and then he began bringing his friends over to share in our little ritual. They all kept the secret ... except one.

As a result of the exposure, I was removed from that home and put into another. This time I was branded as the emotionally unstable slut, whose father killed her mother. I'd learned that keeping the secret wasn't safe, but neither was telling the truth. So I decided to become someone else this time around.

Cilla

The perfect role model presented herself to me when I moved into her room. She was 12 years old and called herself Cilla, short for Priscilla. She'd been in the system since she was six and knew how to get around all the rules. She told me what I needed to do and not do in order to get everything I needed. She taught me to smoke, drink, steal, laugh, and dream. Cilla had no memory of her father and mother and no desire to even discuss the past. She only looked forward to the day she'd be free to follow after her carefully sketched-out plan to make it to the seashore of California. She kept a postcard of a beach in southern California in her drawer. She would pull it out sometimes and we would delight in the thought of visiting such a beautiful place.

For the next two years we dreamed and strategized together until the day our foster mom told us they couldn't keep us anymore. Cilla and I decided we were ready to launch out on our own together. Cilla was 14 years old and I was 12. That night we packed, snuck out the bedroom window, and headed west for the seashore.

Free at Last?

Walking got old real fast, so early in the morning we stopped at a café for breakfast. We had $187 saved up from a little theft and fencing business we engaged in, so we ordered everything we wanted. We were free at last and that breakfast was the best time I'd ever had in my whole life. As we were leaving, a trucker named Bert said he'd seen us walking on the road, and he offered to give us a ride in his truck. My "knower" immediately said No, but Cilla told me not to be a baby and that she wasn't walking anymore. I put on her bravery and followed them to the truck.

I'd never been in one of these big trucks before and was amazed that it had a TV, bed, and refrigerator inside. The trucker offered us both a can of beer and put a video on for us to watch. I kept my eyes on Cilla to see if there was any sense of danger in her eyes. She propped herself up on a pillow, cracked open her beer, and was set to enjoy the ride. I did the same and tried hard to push away the dreadful feeling that was filling my gut.

We drove for miles and soon fell asleep. When I woke up, the truck was stopped outside an old run-down house. I couldn't see the highway anywhere and asked where we were. He told us this was a friend's house and that we could go to the bathroom here while he spoke with his friend.

I followed Cilla's confident stride to the house. Old blankets covered the windows from the inside. Bert's friend opened the door and a sweet-smelling smoke drifted past our noses. His friend was a big man with a big stomach who looked like he'd just run a mile. All he said to us as we followed Bert into the house was, "Yummy." A woman with long black hair was sitting at a table playing with long, white lines of what looked like sugar. She motioned for Cilla and me to have a seat. Cilla asked to use the bathroom and was escorted by Bert's friend. When I proceeded to follow her, the woman grabbed my arm and emphatically told me, "Only one at a time."

Being separated from Cilla panicked me. When I started to protest, someone very big grabbed me from behind, covered my mouth, and carried me to a bedroom. I tried to fight free but was soon surround by two other men who grabbed my arms and legs and pinned me to a bed. When he released my mouth, I tried to call out for Cilla but couldn't find my voice.

Another woman entered the room. Her voice was soft and kind at first, almost hypnotic, as she told me to relax and hold still. I did. She then tied a small rubbery string around my arm and looked hungrily at my veins. "Fresh meat, boys," was the last thing I heard before floating away to sleep.

I didn't know where I was when I woke up. Was I dead? All I could see was a blinding light and my body felt smooth and rubbery. The laughter and voices made me turn my head away from the light. "Welcome back," I heard a male voice growl. I could see the camera now, and realized that I was naked and tied to the bed. They were taking turns as the woman directed them. I had been pretty numb to feelings before, but this level of nothingness was new. I couldn't feel a thing. I closed my eyes and drifted away in my mind to the seashore in Cillas' postcard.

As the months passed, I soon forgot about California and Cilla, who was carted off somewhere else. I had a new friend now who soothed away all physical and emotional pain. Each time the rubber string was put around my arm, she would speak to me from inside my head and tell me everything was going to be OK – that she would never leave me and would always help me forget the abuse and feel better. Her name was Heroin, and by the time I turned 13, I couldn't imagine life without her.

Working the Streets

Our little "family" with its daily routines was soon broken up and I was sold to a man named Clive. Clive drove me to a large city and put me in a run–down hotel with another girl who knew my "good friend," too. We learned to appease Clive's violence with the money we'd bring home from tricking all day on the streets. In return, Clive gave us our daily fixes. As time went by, the next fix became the only thing I lived for, even though the comforting and peaceful feelings it brought were beginning to wane. Heroin's soothing, seductive words had changed to that of an abusive taskmaster, driving me to fix but withholding the pleasure. Her method of operation, like all drugs, was to seduce, addict, and then abuse and control.

I had never known respect from others, so the brandished looks and harsh words of the straight people and cops bounced off me without even a flinch. Most people looked away when they passed by. It wouldn't matter to them if you were lying there bleeding to death. They had simply trained themselves to step over you like a piece of garbage. After all, our own wrong choices got us "scum bags" there, right?

Most people looked away when they passed by. It wouldn't matter to them if you were lying there, bleeding to death. After all, our own wrong choices got us "scum bags" there, right?

Then there were the do-gooders who came by to tell me all about hell and why I was going there if I didn't read their book and follow their rules. I'd heard about their book at my mother's church when I was young. I'd even seen the monster pray its words. I often wondered what the do-gooders did inside their "perfect homes." Being streetwise, I could read them like a book. Most would look at us with shock, disdain, disgust, or outright hatred. A few had learned to paste on their fanned look of concern while they gave us their little speech. I knew they were only there to earn their gold stars in order to go back to their perfect little worlds and tell all their friends what wonderful people they were for reaching out to scum bags like us.

The Smile

Then one day one of these do-gooders passed by and smiled at me. In my entire life I'd never had someone smile at me like that. It was as if she really saw me, as if I was really there and was a person whose life actually mattered. Her eyes danced with love and her smile covered me with what seemed like a warm blanket of acceptance and comfort. I'll never forget that moment as long as I live. This simple genuine smile by a total stranger affected my life forever. That day her dancing eyes and her warm smile imparted to me the knowledge that love existed in this world. I was amazed at the strength of that memory and the peace it would bring each time I replayed it in my mind. It was a magical moment for me and yet it didn't make sense at all to my confused mind. The warm feelings that surfaced in me were foreign. I liked them though I was afraid of them. I soon learned to shove the memory and feelings away when they came to mind, and I carried on with "life." It would be several years before I saw that look of love again.

One Dark Night

It had been an unusually rough night. I'd been picked up by a group of drunken businessmen and was violently raped, beaten, derogated, and thrown out of the car miles from our hotel. I was bloody, bruised, broke, and in desperate need of a hit. I was too sober to take another beating by Clive for not bringing in the cash. I set my mind to do one more trick for a fix before I went home. It was 5 A.M. and I'd have to hurry back to Main Street before the opportunities became too thin.

Main Street was disappointingly empty of both traffic and people, except for a woman who was crossing the street to "talk" to me.

I wasn't in the mood, but the lady's eyes and kind voice stopped me cold. I recognized those eyes; I'd played them over and over again in my mind. The lady was different, but the eyes were the same. They radiated that love I had seen years earlier in the "smile-lady." They looked right past my bloody face and hard façade to the "me" inside that no one ever wanted to know or would even acknowledge existed.

Time seemed to stand still as I faintly heard this woman's words. I was so lost in the love and acceptance of her eyes. I had longed for this love ever since the first day I learned it existed.

"You have had a hard night, haven't you?" the woman asked me. I laughed, "You don't even know the half of it!" Then something strange happened, I felt tears begin to well up in me, tears I hadn't experience in years. I didn't even know I had a tear left in me. I became flushed with weariness and felt my legs begin to buckle.

I was so lost in the love and acceptance of her eyes. I had longed for this love... Then something strange happened, I felt tears well up in me, tears I hadn't experienced in years.

The woman put her hand into her pocket and pulled out a $20 bill. She handed it to me and said, "God loves you and He wants your day to go easier for you today." For some reason I didn't want to lie and so I asked her, "Do you know who I am?" The woman said, "Yes, I know." I responded curtly, as I didn't think she really knew "who" she was giving the money to. "I am an addict! Do you know what I am going to do with this?" The woman answered and said, "Yes, I know."

She further shared, "Precious one, you have so much value. God created you for a great purpose and you are worth much more than what you are experiencing here. God loves you and He wants you free. Your addiction is hurting you, but He is bigger than your addiction and anything else you are facing right now. He can help you, and He will if you let Him. You might go and buy drugs with this money, but what if this will keep you from taking your next trick – the one that might kill you?"

The woman said, "Remember that Jesus loves you very much and will never leave your side. If you call on the name of Jesus, He will be there to help you."

The woman handed me a card that said, "God Loves You with an Everlasting Love." She said, "Keep this with you and remember that He loves you very much and will never leave your side. If you call on the name of Jesus, He will be there to help you." She turned the card over and wrote down a name and address. "Here is the address of a church mission center not far from here where you can get some help. I am only visiting this area and am leaving tomorrow but I know you would be welcomed there." She then prayed for me and asked if she could buy me breakfast. The pain in my body suddenly elevated and called me back to my need for a fix. I politely declined. But that card was to become my lifesaver.

As I walked away, I could feel that something had changed inside me, almost like my feet were no longer trudging through deep mud but were on solid smooth ground. My body was screaming for a fix so I used the money she had given me to "take care of myself" and headed home to sleep. The fix did take the edge off slightly, but it couldn't take me where I'd just been with that lady.

The Turning Point

In the seven years that I was on the street, no one had ever told me I had value or that they loved me. It took me three months to gather the courage to find the church on the back of that card. I sat outside across the street from the store-front mission and watched the people come and go for over a month, not daring to go inside. Eventually, my need for another injection of that love overcame my fear and I went inside.

I tried to share with them what had happened months earlier – that morning with the lady, but I was all confused and couldn't seem to get the words out clearly. Then the tears came again.

Stephanie, a woman in the mission, kindly said, "Sara, you are experiencing God's love. He is reaching out to you and wants to give you a new life – a forever life. You do not have to work for this life. It is a free gift. Jesus is knocking on the door of your heart right now. He would love it if you asked Him to come in and be your personal Savior, Protector, and Provider. He can heal all the wounds of your past. He loves you! You can come to Him just as you are." A floodgate of tears burst forth and I cried uncontrollably. It was as if 19 years of bottled up tears were being released for the very first time. Stephanie hugged me and I fell into her arms while others came around to comfort and encourage me, too. I remained with them all morning and became gloriously born again! I told Stephanie and her husband, Richard, my whole story and they listened without judgment and with such love.

They knew Clive and understood he'd never let me go. Richard made a phone call, and after about half an hour had a plan organized for me to be transported to another community three hours away where a couple involved in a little local church would help me get on my feet. They told me I had to be willing to stay with them for a year and agree to some strict guidelines. Stephanie and Richard assured me that this couple would help me get established in a brand new life in Christ. I finally agreed, with great hesitation to all their terms. It was a difficult decision because I did not how I would cope without my "friend" – Heroin.

I was in rough shape when I arrived later that evening at what would be my new home for the next year. I wanted to run so badly, and yet there was something, or maybe I should say "Someone," enabling me to stay.

Tests and Trials

My first year was not easy. I went through severe drug withdrawal. The "house parents," Art and Lois, along with their church friends, prayed and cared for me, never leaving my side during those hard hours and days. Stephanie would often come to visit and bring encouragement at the most perfect time, and I was on the phone with her almost every day. She gave me strength to continue. There were many things to learn and wrestle through.

Rebellion, lies, manipulation, and hate often manifested in and through me during that year. I had never experienced love until then, so I didn't always know how to receive it, and I definitely did not know how to reciprocate.

Many painful memories surfaced in that intense season. I received much inner healing and deliverance, but the most important thing was that I became acquainted with love. Art, Lois and the church congregation were very patient and kind (most of the time I did test their patience) yet firm when they needed to be. They did not have an easy time in the restoration process, as I did not have any solid foundations in life. I had only known pain, betrayal and lots of reactions – oh yes, lots of reactions! There were many hurdles, mindsets, and reactions to overcome as well as many health issues, but the church was committed spiritually, emotionally, relationally, and financially to me. I attempted to leave a number of times in the first year due to the intensity of the process of restoration. However, in the midst of all my brokenness and challenges, they pulled together, sacrificing their own comforts, to help me come into wholeness.

I obtained my GED (high school graduation equivalent) that year. They taught me to clean house, cook meals, plan nutritious diets, do yard work, and use the computer. My most favorite part of the day was morning devotions where as a family we would worship, pray, and study the Word.

> My most favorite part of the day was morning devotions where as a family we would worship, pray and study the Word. I became acquainted with the Holy Spirt and was astonished by His power and love.

I became acquainted with Holy Spirit and was astonished by His power and love. Every night before I went to sleep, I would read the little card that woman had given me on the street early that morning: "God Loves You with an Everlasting Love." I would be eternally grateful to both her and the woman the Lord initially used to bring His love into my dark world with her smile and kindness.

After the first year, I remained in the community and got my first job. It was twenty-five hours per week working in the laundry and housekeeping department of a local day care center. I eventually got hired full time, moved into my own place and continued to grow in Christ. Every year I overcame obstacles and grew more and more into the woman God meant for me to be.

Back to the Streets

After being in restoration for three and a half years, Stephanie asked if I would like to join her and Richard on an outreach in front of their mission center on Friday night that week. They were planning on serving free hot chocolate and sandwiches to the homeless and drug addicted in their area. This was the area I used to turn tricks in. This was where I shot up on heroin. What would it be like to go back? Was I strong enough? Stephanie and I prayed together and we both felt that it was the timing of the Lord.

Friday night came quicker than I wanted it to. My ride was coming soon and I was standing in front of the mirror looking at a woman who had been transformed. I thought back to my life on the streets only a few years previously and it seemed so foreign to me. What a gift to feel the dramatic separation from those days.

On our way to the inner city district we passed many familiar places that were part of my old life – hotels, bars, and restaurants. I saw girls seductively pacing back and forth on the street corners and in front of the clubs looking for tricks. It broke my heart. What was their story? How did they get there? Tears streamed down my cheeks. I had so much compassion for them. I was now free, but what about them? What about them?

We parked in a lot a couple of streets behind the mission and walked towards the stand that was set up in front of the center. Again, my heart broke as I looked at the devastation around me. Suddenly, I felt so inadequate. I knew the possible history behind each vacant gaze, but what could I do to help? I gave out hot chocolate and sandwiches but it seemed like nothing in comparison to the help they actually needed. The Holy Spirit whispered into my thoughts. "Smile... just smile." I remembered how a simple smile began to change the course of my life. So I did just that. I smiled and smiled and smiled!

> The Holy Spirit whispered into my thoughts. "Smile... just smile." I remembered how a simple smile began to change the course of my life. So I did just that. I smiled and smiles and smiled!

Every homeless, addicted individual who came to the table to receive some food and beverage that night received a smile from me. I looked right into their eyes and allowed my heart to say, "You have so much value." To some I mustered up the boldness to declare over their confused and tormented lives, "God loves you with an everlasting love." And then... I smiled some more.

Overdosed

That was the beginning of regular outreaches to the streets. One night after giving out hot chocolate, Stephanie and Richard and I walked down a dark alley where I had often shot up years earlier. A prostitute was sprawled out on the deteriorated pavement as many walked by her. When you live on the streets you do not really matter to anyone. Many girls went missing or died from overdose and seldom did anyone come looking for them. I stooped down next to this woman. She had overdosed but she was still breathing. Stephanie and Richard helped me get her back to the mission and we cared for her over the next number of hours. She wanted to go back to the streets as soon as she was able, but I knew that maybe one day she would change her mind. I gave her a little card that I had printed. I had printed thousands of them for my ministry on the streets. It said on the front, "God Loves YOU with an Everlasting Love." On the back of the card was the address of Stephanie and Richard's church mission. Maybe one day, she would have the courage to come back – one day.

My Life Filled with Purpose

I was rescued in order to rescue others. I am blessed in order to be a blessing. I truly love my new life, but my journey to wholeness continues to be a daily walk of faith. It isn't always easy for me to respond in a godly manner to daily challenges and situations, and trust is still difficult at times. I have learned to take one day at a time. The mercies of God are new every morning. I know that I am forgiven by a loving Savior who took my sin and brokenness upon Himself two thousand years ago. I know that I know, that I know, that He truly does love me with an everlasting love!

Sara had no one to love or care for her as a child, teenager, or young woman. She was neglected, abandoned, and abused year after year. Her heart was hardened and her ways were rebellious. Only God could see the well of tears stored up within her heart, for she didn't dare let anyone know she was hurting. She was alone, afraid, and hurting beyond belief ... but now, so rescued.

Beautiful, beautiful, Sara – you are so precious and deeply loved. **For your tears He died! Yes, for your tears He died!**

This chapter, by Patricia King and Shirley Ross of XPmedia, is a composite of three true stories. Names, places and some details have been changed in order to protect identities.

And while he was still a long way off, his father saw him coming. Filled with love and compassion, he ran to his son, embraced him, and kissed him.

His father said to the servants... "We must celebrate with a feast, for this son of mine was dead and has now returned to life. He was lost, but now he is found." So the party began.

Luke 15:20, 22-24 (NLT)

DIVINE APPOINTMENTS
Joshua's Story

Joshua lived in a lower-middle class suburb of Los Angeles. Both his parents were heroin addicts, but there was no hint of this if you drove through his neighborhood. Their home, like others on the street, though small and simple, appeared to be well kept and orderly. The home was clean with humble furnishings.

Joshua's father worked at a car-parts yard that was also a front for a fencing operation that he was part of. In addition, he was a drug dealer and he acted as "agent" for his wife, who "entertained" men in their home in order to support her habit. Not every night but most, she would host one or two men in her bedroom. Joshua and his little sister were to be seen and not heard. If they were still up, they sat orderly on the sofa in the living room watching television. They saw men go into her room and then leave a short time later.

Neither of Joshua's parents had gone to high school or trade school. Although his parents used discretion when they "shot up," little Joshua did see his parents use drugs from time to time and witnessed them being sick occasionally due to drug withdrawal and overdose. The house, although clean and orderly in the natural, was filled with an atmosphere of fear and control. It didn't take much for his parents to get into full-fledged fights accompanied by yelling, screaming, threats, and sometimes mild physical assaults. If the children misbehaved or spoke out of turn, the punishment was severe. They were to behave at all times and at all costs.

When Joshua was five and a half years of age, his father was arrested on federal charges and sentenced to prison. His mother was left to support her habit and look after the household needs. Within the year they were evicted from their home because she had neglected to pay the rent.

The day they left their home, Joshua pulled his little roller bag packed with his favorite bed toy (a plush lion he called Leo), some Lego blocks, pajamas, and his Flintstone toothbrush. They moved into a ground-floor apartment in the Rampart District of L.A. His mother entered full-fledged, full-time prostitution in order to support her habit. She often entertained men at home during the day, and most nights she was on the streets. But that was not all.

She also started selling Joshua and his sister to men for sexual favors so she could support her habit. Men would come to their apartment and Joshua and his sister would have to perform oral sex. Then they paid his mother and left. Joshua remembers at times two men in the room together, one with his sister and one with him – both at the same time. Joshua hated it but was not allowed to complain. After all, his mother would remind them, "Children are to be seen and not heard." The Rampart District was full of crime and murder. It was a dangerous place to live. Joshua was often overcome by fear, but who could he tell? He was warned to keep the "family secrets."

Nine months after they moved, his little sister contracted severe pneumonia and fever. One night she was delirious with fever and was struggling to breathe. Joshua was alone with her, not knowing what to do. Frightened and help-less, he finally ran next door for help and the neighbor came over. Right at that moment his mother came through the door with one of her clients. She was upset that Joshua had let someone into the apartment. He was scared but held back the tears. The neighbor and his mother entered into a violent argument. Finally, the neighbor in the heat of the argument grabbed the phone and called 911. An ambulance arrived within the hour while the mother and the neighbor were still yelling at each other. Joshua remained silent.

> Joshua's mother started selling him and his sister to men for sexual favors so she could support her habit. Joshua hated it but was not allowed to complain. After all, his mother would remind him, "Children are to be seen and not heard."

His sister was taken to the hospital but died in the emergency room. Joshua was alone in the apartment while his mother was at the hospital with his sister. When she came home she was very angry with him. No reason – just angry. He curled up in his bed that night with Leo. He wanted to cry, but he couldn't. He wanted to say something, but what? And who would listen anyway?

Miss Jennifer, Joshua's teacher at school, took a keen interest in him. She loved him and cared about how the death of his sister affected him. She often invited him to stay after class for a while and help her. She gave him after-school treats and encouraged him. He mainly listened. He was most often tongue-tied, but he loved being in her presence. She told him how smart he was and that if he finished school he could have a great future when he was older. He loved school and wished he could live there. Sometimes he would draw a special picture for Miss Jennifer and color it with his crayons. She always enjoyed receiving his pictures and that made him feel good inside. One day he picked a flower for her and was delighted when she thanked him for it, saying how much she liked it.

He loved Miss Jennifer and she played a big role in his life by speaking encouragement and potential into him. It was at that time, thanks to her influence, that Joshua made two decisions: first, he decided to never become a drug addict, and secondly, he would graduate from high school (making him the first in his family to graduate).

He was always happy when he was with Miss Jennifer, but the joy waned as he approached home. When he arrived back at the apartment, his mother was seldom there. When she was home, she was often either sick or agitated with withdrawal symptoms, or she was getting ready for a client – either her own or one she had lined up for Joshua.

One day after school as Joshua opened the door to the apartment, there was a lady waiting for him whom he had never met before. She was dressed in plain, clean but colorful clothing, a lot like Miss Jennifer – not like the way his mom dressed. She was kind and gentle, but she bore difficult news. Joshua's mother had been arrested on prostitution and drug possession charges. The lady was a social worker. She explained that he would have to stay with his grandparents who lived in Riverside. Joshua didn't know them well since they severely disapproved of their daughter's lifestyle and had distanced themselves from her and their grandchildren when Joshua's dad was put into prison.

Joshua had to leave immediately. He was so sad as he thought about Miss Jennifer! How could he let her know where he was going? When could he see her again? He felt tears well up, but they wouldn't flow. Once again he left with his little roller bag, now missing a wheel. Leo was tucked away inside along with a photograph of Miss Jennifer and him on his first field trip. Oh, how he would miss her.

Broken Promises

It was supposed to be a temporary situation, but Joshua remained with his grandparents for the rest of his childhood. Miss Jennifer found out where he lived and was given permission to see him. The first time she came to visit, his heart felt like it was going to pound right out of his chest! She gave him such a sense of comfort, and she brought him some treats. She visited him about five times in the first year, but then the visits grew fewer and fewer. By age twelve he never heard from her again, but he never forgot her.

He occasionally saw his mother, but she never changed her lifestyle. She was in and out of jail and continued to use the needle and engage in prostitution. Joshua didn't see his father again until many years later when he visited him in prison.

Joshua's grandparents looked after him well. He was fed, clothed, educated, and had a stable home from the time he went to live with them when he was eight. He was never sexually exploited again, but he never told anyone what had happened to him. He was determined to graduate from high school and he studied hard. He continued to be determined to never use drugs. Joshua was a good boy. He was quiet and had only one friend – Brandon. He mainly kept to himself, but whenever Brandon would ask him to do something, he would. They rode their bikes together, played video games, and sometimes watched movies.

In their sophomore year, Brandon got involved in the party lifestyle at school and started using drugs. Joshua would go with him to the parties but was uncomfortable. He refused to use drugs but did drink some beer and sometimes some hard liquor. He got drunk once and threw up all over the bathroom floor. He did not like drinking or getting drunk. He did not drink again after that.

Brandon was using drugs more and more. Joshua was concerned for him but was unable to give him a clear warning. He just couldn't get the words out.

In his senior year, Brandon overdosed and died. At the funeral, Joshua felt such deep pain and remorse, but once again he couldn't cry or speak. This time, though, something new happened. He felt rage rise up within his heart. He was so angry! He felt it. It was real, strong, and uncontrollable. Never had he identified this intense and all-encompassing emotion before. He ran out of the funeral home and punched a wall over and over until his fist was bleeding and swollen. Some of Brandon's friends had a party after the funeral. He went with them. Everyone was doing drugs and drinking. And this time, Joshua did drugs, too, no longer caring about the promises he had made to himself. What was the use?

Joshua fell in love with cocaine the first time he did it and stayed high for days. He didn't go home; he didn't want to. His grandparents were worried about him but he didn't care. The violent anger within continued to manifest. He got involved in a number of fights. He had never hurt anyone before, but now he couldn't stop. He wanted to, but he couldn't. He

He felt rage rise within his heart. He was so angry! He felt it. It was real, strong, and uncontrollable. Never had he identified this intense and self-encompassing emotion before.

hated what he was doing, but the rage kept surfacing. It controlled him. Tim, one of Brandon's friends who was at the party, was a gang member and started hanging out with Joshua. Joshua met a few more of the members and hung out at parties with them. They got into some fights together and before long Joshua was officially initiated into the gang. Three months before graduation he was expelled from school due to truancy. He did not graduate – another broken promise to himself.

He left his grandparents home and was sucked into the vortex of violence and drug abuse. Within the next year, he was a hardcore gang member and criminal. Joshua was very angry and full of hate.

Two years went by and his life was getting very dark. He had to stay high in order to tolerate the pain, guilt, and shame that haunted him continuously. Nightmares tormented him almost every night and he always had a hard time sleeping. He took downers in order to sleep, and eventually started shooting heroin. Joshua was addicted.

He felt hopeless, angry, depressed, and suicidal. Heroin took the edge off sometimes, but the hopelessness always lingered. Late one night he went to his dealer's house and purchased enough drugs to kill himself. He drove into the Rampart District and parked in front of the school where he had met Miss Jennifer years earlier. He walked around the school building and found a little alcove at the bottom of a cement staircase. He sat there for a while, reminiscing of his time at this school. Like a ticker tape, his life was played out in his mind. As he reviewed all the pain, trauma, abuse, and disappointments, he felt more hopeless than ever. His dream of graduating from high school and never using drugs were now gone. What was there to live for?

"Miss Jennifer said that I could do well in life. She said that I was smart. Ha! Look at me now, Miss Jennifer. Look at me now!"

Just as the sun was starting to rise on the horizon, he shot up everything he had in the stairway alcove at the side of the school. This was the place he chose to die. He intentionally overdosed that morning, curled up in the staircase alcove against the school-house basement door, and intended to never wake up.

Moments later two police officers came by to check out the school. They were suspicious because of the car parked out front and wondered if there was a break-in. Flashlights in hand, they walked around the building and found Joshua curled up against the door at the bottom of the stairs. They shook him, realizing that he had overdosed. The released tourniquet was still hanging on his sleeve and the used needle lay beside him. Blood was running down his arm. One of the police officers was a Christian. While shaking him and calling out for him to wake up, he prayed a prayer of desperation for him, "Lord Jesus, save him. Deliver him. Please Lord, don't let him die." His partner seemed quite comfortable with the prayer even though he did not practice the Christian faith. Immediately after the prayer, Joshua miraculously came to. Instantaneously, he felt completely sober, but didn't want to. He wanted to die! What was going on?

"God has a plan for your life that is good. Don't give up," exhorted the Christian officer."

They stood him up. He was breathing normally and able to stand on his own. "We have to write up this report, young man, and I also want to make sure that you are OK," explained the Christian officer. The other officer seemed to be in agreement.

Joshua was quiet – very quiet – and compliant. There was a strange peace that filled him. He knew it was not the affects of the drugs – this feeling was different. There was no agitation, only clarity and peace. It was the same feeling he used to have when he was with Miss Jennifer.

They escorted him over to the police vehicle and put him in the back seat. They sat together in the vehicle in front of the school for what seemed like a long time and wrote up the report. There were a number of calls back and forth to the police station, but Joshua was oblivious to it all. He was enjoying the peace. "What is this peace?" he wondered.

The Christian officer, whose name was Michael, asked him, "How are you feeling?"

"I'm feeling great," Joshua responded.

Michael's partner got off a call and said, "Well, boy, we have good news for you. We are not going to charge you with anything. You are free to go."

Joshua was somewhat shocked but got up to leave, grabbing his jacket. Then Michael put his arm around his shoulder and whispered, "Hey, man, I am getting off my shift in about 45 minutes. If you wait here in your car, I will come by and we can talk."

Joshua said nothing but slowly and peacefully walked over to his car, sat in the driver's seat, wrapped his arms around the wheel and rested his head on his arms. He drifted off to sleep as the police car drove away.

An Open Door and a New Day

"Joshua! Joshua!"

Joshua woke up hearing his name called. Forgetting where he was for a moment, he came out of a deep sleep, looked up, and saw Michael banging on the car window trying to get his attention.

Joshua opened the door, and that was the beginning of the rest of his life.

Michael took Joshua for breakfast at a nearby café and then invited him back to his place. He lived in a small house that he shared with Geoff, a roommate, not far from the Rampart District. Both Geoff and Michael were born-again Christians. That morning they shared the Gospel with Joshua. The presence of God flooded the kitchen of their home where they were sitting, and Joshua that morning was gloriously born again. Michael and Geoff invited him to stay with them in their extra room. They moved a desk into the living room and made the den into a bedroom for Joshua.

By early evening, Joshua started feeling sick. Drug withdrawal symptoms were setting in and getting stronger as the evening went on, yet he had no desire to find drugs to alleviate his discomfort and agitation. Even though he physically felt terrible, he was experiencing a deep inner peace at the same time. This was very unusual. He had experienced withdrawal before and it was never like this.

The next few days were very difficult, but the peace remained. Geoff and Michael, along with Michael's fiancé, Shelly, took shifts looking after him. One of them was always there and they had friends from their house-church group come in to pray, also. They played worship music and the Bible on CD all day and all night. The withdrawal symptoms were brutal, but in the midst of it the peace of the Lord remained and strengthened him.

The Holy Spirit gave him a number of dreams and an open vision during that time. At first he wondered if it was the effects of the drugs that had been in his system, but the encounters were so amazing they had to be from God. During the most difficult time of withdrawal, he was baptized in the Holy Spirit and began to speak in tongues. He used his prayer language a lot and when he did, the symptoms waned. After a few days he started to feel stronger and was able to eat. The worship music and the Bible verses were a delight to him.

> The withdrawal symptoms were brutal, but in the midst of it the peace of the Lord remained and strengthened Him.

Michael bought him his first Bible – it was a *Living Bible* and he loved it. He read it by the hour and received revelation from the Spirit of Truth. He loved worship and would sing along with the worship music on the CDs.

Michael, Shelly, and Geoff were part of a vibrant, Spirit-filled house church. Joshua joined in the meetings and fellowship every time they gathered. He enjoyed those times and loved listening to the testimonies and teachings of those who attended. He felt so much love there! Usually an addict has cravings for their drugs when they come off, but all his cravings were gone from the moment Michael and the other officer rescued him at the school. It was a divine intervention.

He performed yard and household chores for Michael and Geoff in order to cover his room and board, and he spent time with the Lord constantly. He loved his new life. He had become a true man of God. Six months passed and he was growing in passion for Christ by the day. He had even joined the evangelism teams and was winning souls for Christ. He signed up for a program in order to get his graduation certificate. He was doing well.

One day while out for a long walk, he discovered his old neighborhood in the Rampart District. He sat down on a bus bench across the street from the apartment building that he lived in as a child with his mother and sister. All the memories came flooding back – the terrible abuse, the death of his sister, his mother's drug addiction, the loneliness, the abandonment ... and the sexual exploitation ... oh, yes, the sexual exploitation. How could he have forgotten that? He had never been able to shed a tear for any of it. The tears were all bottled up. But, as he sat there, the flood gate opened and the tears flowed like a river. He couldn't stop crying. There he was, sitting on the bus bench with traffic driving by and people passing, some stopping to stare and inquire if he was alright. He couldn't answer. He just kept crying.

He sat on the bench crying for over an hour that day. It was like the weight of the world lifted off his shoulders. Over the next number of months he received inner healing ministry and deliverance and was taught even more about the Father's love. Layers and layers of pain were peeled off and healed. It was glorious!

Joshua was easy to disciple. He had met Jesus in a very powerful way and he was not going to let go. As easy as it was, though, the first year was not without its challenges. Michael and Shelly got married and moved to the other side of town. As a result he seldom saw them and he had to fight the fear of abandonment. Geoff worked the night shift at the hospital and, as a result, left Joshua alone most nights. He still suffered bad dreams from time to time and had to learn to overcome those night terrors.

When Joshua visited his grandparents and eagerly told them about his new life in Christ, they became upset and angry with him. They resented religion and believed Joshua was being deceived. This confused Joshua, and once again he felt the pain of rejection. They handed him two boxes of personal belongings and told him to go make a life for himself. When he got home and opened the boxes, there was his little roller bag with the broken wheel. Leo was in the box, also, along with the photograph of him and Miss Jennifer. The items brought back a flood of bad memories, so he took everything in the boxes and disposed of it – even Leo and the photo of Miss Jennifer.

One of the hardest things he faced towards the end of that year was that the house fellowship disbanded due to striving and jealousies.

On the heels of Michael and Shelly moving, being alone at night, his grandparents rejecting him, and the church disbanding, he fell for a young woman. But when he invited her out, she was rude and cruelly rejected him. It was all too much. He was shattered. Unfortunately, he made some wrong decisions. He connected with an old friend from the gang and spent a weekend partying with him. He got high on some drugs they offered and the violence surfaced. He partied for two days without sleep, and his emotions were raw.

Geoff knew something was wrong and called Michael, Shelly, and a couple of other friends who helped to disciple Joshua. They looked high and low for him but couldn't find him. They prayed and asked others who were part of a prayer chain to pray that they find him. Late one night as they were driving through a McDonald's drive-through, they noticed three guys in a fight in the corner of the parking lot. One guy was standing back watching, one was on the ground, and the other on top of him pounding him. They ran over and grabbed the guy who was doing all the pounding. Michael grabbed him and pulled him off with force, saying, "Hey! Enough! Cool down!" He looked at the young man's face in order to speak more directly to him, and to his shock it was Joshua.

"Joshua! Joshua!" he said, "What are you doing? This is not who you are. You are a man of God!

"Joshua! Joshua! What are you doing? This is not who you are! You are a man of God! You are a man of God!" Michael then broke down with Joshua in his grip and wept saying, "I love you, man! Let's go home. Let's go home."

Joshua did go home — with his true friends that night. Behold, what manner of love is this? Joshua continued to grow in the love of God. He went on to take a college computer course that year and met the girl of his dreams while in school. She was raised in a Christian home, had never done drugs, had never back-slidden, and was a virgin when they met. He married her. Joshua got a good job in the computer field and his wife taught preschool in a local elementary school complex.

One day she came home excited and said, "Joshua, do you know a woman by the name of Jennifer Martin Hack?"

"No, Hon', I don't think so," he answered.

"Well, she knows you. She noticed my last name and asked me if I was married to a Joshua. She taught you in first and second grade."

"Jennifer Martin Hack? What? You mean ... Miss Jennifer?"

Thanks to a God-designed turn of events, Joshua was able to get re-acquainted with Miss Jennifer!

In all the lonely, agonizing, painful, and abusive moments, hours, days, and years, Christ's hand was outstretched to Joshua. The Lord never left him. His love eye was always watching over him and saw every bottled up tear that he couldn't release. His ear was attentive to every silent cry that no one else heard.

Joshua, you are so loved and cherished. We are all thankful for the great deliverance you encountered and for the testimony of His love you carry. **It was for your tears He died!**

This chapter, by Patricia King and Shirley Ross of XPmedia, is based on a true story. Names, places and some details have been slightly changed in order to protect identities.

[Jesus] felt compassion for them because they were like

sheep without a shepherd;

and He began to teach them many things.

Mark 6:34

LOST AND FOUND

ON AMERICA'S STREETS

Three Stories

A Troubled Teen - Jessica's Story

On the night sixteen-year-old Jessica disappeared, she was last seen at a party her mother forbade her to attend. Later that evening she called her mom begging her to come pick her up, but her mom was too upset to respond. Unfortunately, this was the last Tracy heard of her daughter for the next weeks to come. That night Jessica was abducted, beaten, and gang-raped.

For weeks Jessica's captors kept her hostage in an apartment in one of Phoenix's most dangerous neighborhoods. After days of physical and mental abuse, they forced her to dress up, then took a picture of her and placed her on craigslist. Shortly after the ad posted, men began to arrive. Each of them pleasured themselves at the expense of Jessica's innocence.

Although she had been deeply wounded and abused, Jessica still managed to maintain the hope of escaping. Through patience, she led her captors to believe that she was fully "broken" so they let their guard down, allowing her to move about freely in the apartment. This was when she seized the opportunity and escaped through the bathroom window.

She took her daughter to the police to report the kidnapping, rape, assault and attempted murder on her daughter's life. To their shock and dismay, the police officer dismissed their case for lack of evidence.

Jessica headed directly to her parents' home and explained everything that had happened to her since the night she was abducted. Her father refused to believe her, but her mother did. Tracy was heart-broken and filled with anger toward these men who had violently abused her daughter. She took her daughter to the police to report the kidnapping, rape, assault, and attempted murder on her daughter's life.

Once in the safety of the police station, Tracy recounted all that Jessica had shared. To their shock and dismay, the police officer attending to them dismissed their case for lack of evidence. He also accused Jessica of making up the stories as an alibi to running away. They were sent home without an investigation.

Eventually, Jessica returned to school, but her pimp began stalking her daily. He taunted her as he drove around the campus, professing ownership of her. She told her mother, and Tracy did her best to protect her daughter. But being unarmed, inexperienced, and alone, Tracy was unprepared for the day Jessica was kidnapped again.

This time she was taken by force from her school's premises. While Tracy was attempting to file another police report for her missing daughter, Jessica was being trafficked out of their jurisdiction to Florida.

Girls like Jessica are considered a flight risk in the trafficking industry. Therefore, she had to be "shipped" far away from her hometown. Girls can be sold for as little as $50 a person, but her pimp had set up a trade instead.

Upon arrival in Florida, Jessica was traded in. Once in the hands of her new "owner," Jessica was branded. As farmers brand their cows, a hot iron seared the back of Jessica's neck with the words, "Property of ___."

From then on, Jessica lost all hope of returning to her family. She was now someone's property and asset. She submitted to the authority that now governed her and ran the streets as she was expected to do, turning over all her earnings to the pimp. Some nights she hardly got to eat. She was overwhelmed as she tried to meet her nightly quota while avoiding cops and staying safe.

After a couple of years, Jessica was arrested and held in police custody. The police officers investigated and uncovered Jessica's terrifying story. They contacted her mother in Arizona, but had to, by law, keep her in a lock-down facility. She was not yet 18.

Arrested underage prostitutes are kept in juvenile facilities in an effort to protect them from the pimps who lurk around outside awaiting their return. There aren't many alternative lodgings for these girls, so upon completion of their time, they are eventually released back onto the streets.

Fortunately, after her time in the juvenile facility, Jessica was placed in a rehabilitation center. Although Tracy and Jessica have been deeply scarred by these occurrences, they have found comfort and restoration through an abundant life in Jesus Christ, the Ultimate Healer. Tracy and Jessica now minister to others, sharing their testimony of how God restores. Her story is shared by many organizations that offered support and prayers throughout their painful journey.

By the year of Jessica's release, the answer to prayers had already manifested through the arrest of Jessica's pimp, a notorious gang-banger and trafficker. He was arrested, charged, and is now serving time in government custody. Unchained Generation (UG) is one of the many Christian organizations that extended a hand of hope to Tracy during her daughter's absence.

A Broken Spirit - Natalie's Story

Every night Natalie sat in her car weeping profusely as she prepared for another night on the "pole." It wasn't too long ago that she lived the American dream. Her husband was in a seminary, preparing for ministry, her kids were well, and their needs were met. She still couldn't understand how she ended up here, but she remembered when it all happened.

Her husband had successfully hidden his addiction until it had gotten out of control. Natalie watched in shock as her entire life crumbled before her eyes. Her husband's job and prospective career in ministry were being traded for his temporary absence of sobriety. Their relationship had totally shattered and the kids were beginning to feel the consequences.

Natalie glared at the neon lights as the clients arrived. She hated the scent of their alcohol breath and wished they would not touch her. They were dirty, vulgar, and disrespectful. What was entertainment for them was torture for her, as every word spoken to her represented a life she wished she had never embraced. She felt trapped and blemished for life. She didn't want to be there.

She also drank a lot now. She refused to go into that place sober. She couldn't. She finished the entire bottle of hard liquor she kept in her car, and then headed to pay for the night. Every dancer had to pay the club to work there. In addition to that, she had to pay a percentage of her tips to the "house" and the bouncers.

Once she entered the doors of the club, she lost all dignity. No one treated her with care or respect. She was a product and a toy, expected to step onto the stage and perform.

It was close to Christmas and Natalie couldn't stop worrying about her kids this year. She had just settled herself in the tiny dressing room she shared with over 20 girls when the bouncer walked in. He announced that the "church ladies" were coming in.

Natalie had once been a "church lady" herself. She felt like the prodigal son who had gone in search of a better life. Was her Heavenly Father awaiting her with a feast as well?

As soon as Natalie heard this, she knew they were coming for her. A mixture of hope and embarrassment flooded her soul. The other girls didn't seem bothered. They shared that these crazy church ladies came by every Christmas to bring gifts and goodies.

Natalie had once been a "church lady" herself. She had fallen and was now trapped in this dark world. She felt like the prodigal son who had gone astray in search of a better life. Was her Heavenly Father awaiting her with a feast, as well?

103

As the ladies arrived, Natalie was quite surprised to see that they weren't dressed in long churchy dresses with matching hats and shoes. Instead, they were dressed like ordinary young women on their way to the movies or dinner. These ladies confidently walked into the dressing room with genuine smiles on their faces – not one condemning look.

One in particular, Courtney, walked over to Natalie and handed her a beautifully decorated gift bag filled with perfume, lotion, nail polish and a pretty pink Bible. She sat next to Natalie. Her presence brought much peace, and Natalie's heart flooded with emotions.

She opened up and told Courtney everything about her life. She didn't hold back and, for once in a very long time, she actually felt that someone cared. Courtney hugged her and prayed with her, sharing words of encouragement. That night Natalie rededicated her life to the Lord. "Tonight the Lord sent me an angel," she told Courtney. This was the last night Natalie drove into the club to work.

Courtney and the other women are from Unchained Generation, and they fervently prayed for Natalie after the encounter. Three months later, Natalie contacted Courtney to let her know that she had quit stripping that night and was now working toward restoring the relationship with her family.

Lost In a Foreign Land - Tina's Story

The day was Chinese New Year. It had been ten years since Tina left her home in China. Chasing dreams and empty promises, Tina had left her only son in Beijing. She was deceived, misled, used, and abused. She was now trapped in a life she didn't want – in a foreign land, forced to do things she was ashamed of. She had no family here and barely spoke the language. She was at the mercy of her "manager."

It was nighttime and the clients started to trickle in. Very few clients actually came to get a massage. Most knew what was really being sold behind the locked doors. Knowing the consequences of getting caught in such a place, those customers parked far away from the shop. Most clients were men, but there were some rare instances where women came to solicit services. Usually those women came alone.

It had been ten years since Tina left her home in China. Chasing dreams and empty promises, she was now trapped in a life she didn't want in a foreign land, forced to do things she was ashamed of.

This is why the four ladies who appeared at the door took Tina aback. These women seemed clueless as they strolled in with big smiles, a basket, and some gift bags. "No buy!" she said to discourage any marketing in the lobby, but the ladies insisted. "We're not selling anything. Happy Chinese New Year!" they exclaimed. They even had an interpreter who spoke Chinese.

When Tina realized what they were saying, her heart sank. She had totally forgotten the celebration that accompanied the Chinese holiday. Here, they were still made to work regardless of the day. Now, these strange women had ignorantly come in with gifts. She wasn't sure how to respond. She bowed in appreciation, then sat to inspect a gift bag. No one ever brought her anything. She felt unworthy.

These women sat and talked with Tina. She told them about her son. It was obvious she longed for her boy. They told her about a Savior, Jesus, who died so that all could be free. Another younger girl peaked out curiously to see the gifts. She stood by and listened as the Gospel was shared. Another client came in and was quickly escorted behind the locked doors. Tina stayed. She wished they could stay but her manager was there, monitoring everything. The ladies had to leave, so they gathered and prayed. Never had Tina felt so close to God.

The ladies left the parlor that night, but in spirit they were with Tina. Two of those ladies were from Unchained Generation. They met weekly to intercede on behalf of Tina and others in bondage. The effective fervent prayer of a righteous man avails much. In less than three months, that massage parlor was among twenty illegal massage parlors in a human trafficking bust.

Unchained Generation

The grim reality of sex trafficking has swept through many places in the western world, but the Lord, our God, is mighty to save. He has dispatched an army to protect the innocent, to take what the locusts have stolen, and to restore what was once plundered.

Many ministries and individuals are following God's heart, loosening chains through the power of Jesus Christ and His love – soul by soul, heart by heart, touching lives, restoring hope, and facilitating godly justice.

Though hundreds of victims have yet to be found, many are being rescued, and some have been restored through the power and love of Jesus Christ. They live among us as vessels of God's honor. They survived and now live to fight for the freedom of those they left behind. These are their stories. Jesus loves them and rescued them, **because for their tears He died!**

These stories, written by Amber Dolson, president and founder of Unchained Generation, represent true accounts. For more information about Unchained Generation, and to learn how you can become involved, visit their website Unchainedgeneration.com.

PART THREE:
Choices of Desperation

Internet sites and brochures that promote cities and countries known for their sex tourism show pictures of people with smiling faces, and allude to "women who are eager to please" and other enticing pleasures. But behind this façade are very different stories. The following accounts are from three people who entered into prostitution because they saw it as the only way they could survive or support their families.

A sex tourist, defending himself, said, "I can assure you this life is a lot better for these girls than working in the rice fields." I replied, "Do you know what one of the girls told me the other night? She said, 'I want to die. I would rather die and go to hell than do this.'"
–Annie Diesselberg, NightLight, Bangkok

While women weep, as they do now, I'll fight; while children go hungry, as they do now, I'll fight; while men go to prison, in and out, in and out, as they do now, I'll fight; while there is a drunkard left, while there is a poor lost girl upon the streets, while there remains one dark soul without the light of God, I'll fight – I'll fight to the very end! –*William Booth*

CHOICES OF DESPERATION
The Stories

And there was a woman in the city who was a sinner ... and standing behind Him at His feet, weeping, she began to wet His feet with her tears, and kept wiping them with the hair of her head, and kissing His feet and anointing them with the perfume.

Now when the Pharisee who had invited Him saw this, he said to himself, "If this man were a prophet He would know who and what sort of person this woman is who is touching Him, that she is a sinner."

[Then Jesus said] "For this reason I say to you, her sins, which are many, have been forgiven, for she loved much; but he who is forgiven little, loves little."

Luke 7:37-39, 47

THE TRAGEDY BEHIND
A FORCED SMILE
Koy's Story

*I*f you had happened upon Koy in the red light district of Bangkok several years ago, she would have probably been smiling – not because she was happy doing what she did, but because she needed the money. The happy face was a deceiving façade to make men choose her and believe the lie that the young women actually enjoy what they do.

The truth is that beneath every smiling bargirl you see in the red light districts of Bangkok, Pattaya, and any other city in Southeast Asia, there is a heart-wrenching story of despair, shame, depression, addiction, and so much more.

When Koy was born in the village of Trat, Thailand, there was no celebration, no excitement. Her mother became very ill, and within a month of her daughter's birth, she died. All of her life, Koy wondered, "What would it have been like to know my mother? What did her face look like?"

Her brokenhearted father realized he needed someone to care for his little baby girl, so he remarried very soon. But in a short time, his new wife became pregnant. When their little boy was born, all the love and attention was focused on him. There was no doubt in little Koy's mind that they loved him more -much more- than they loved her or her older brother.

Koy noticed how her little half-brother - and other kids in the village, for that matter - received praise and hugs from their parents. But Koy grew up starving for love and affirmation, longing to hear that she was a good daughter and that they were pleased with her. Instead, she received scoldings or no attention at all. The love never came.

Nevertheless, Koy had a dream: To study, achieve some kind of career, and make a good living for herself and her family. This is what good daughters did - earn money so they could help support their parents. There were few options for village girls, but she really did hope to go to a school that would prepare her for a decent job later on. However, when she finished her basic sixth grade education, her parents told her they didn't have enough money to further her studies and, like every honorable daughter, it was time for her to go to Bangkok to start earning money for the family. Koy was 13.

§

When Koy arrived in Bangkok, she started working as a seamstress with friends from the same village. The hours were long, she was paid little, and the work was hard - but it was a much better option than what so many other girls from the village did – work in the bars and brothels.

There was also that void crying out to her – the need to love and be loved cleaved deeply in her heart. After a few years in the city, she met someone and fell in love with him. She gave her all to him and soon became pregnant. A short time later, however, they broke up and he left her to fend for herself and her baby on her own. What was she to do? Her sewing job didn't provide enough to send money to her family, which was still considered her obligation, and at the same time take care of her own new small family. She went back to her village and left her baby boy with her parents so she wouldn't have to worry about him while she worked. But it didn't help matters much. She still had one extra mouth to feed.

By then Koy had made friends with several bargirls and they began trying to convince her to go work with them. "You will make a lot more money if you work at the bars," several told her. Even though she knew it was true, the idea filled her with dread. But her struggles increased and it was hard not to be swayed by those enticing her. Finally, her friends convinced her to go check it out. "Money – lots of money. That's what I need to ease my troubles," she thought. Maybe she could work the bar without actually having to sleep with the customers. One of the main activities the girls did was go-go dancing – dancing sensuously and clothed scantily for leering foreign men. She dreaded even the though of that. But perhaps, just perhaps, she could avoid actually having to go away with the *farangs* – the Thai term for foreigners.

However, after a month of doing the bar and partying circuit with her friends, she had to face the truth. At the bars, there was only one way to make real money. In fact, bargirls' salaries are docked if they don't satisfy a specified monthly "quota." The thought of doing it left her embarrassed and ashamed. One thing was being with the person you loved. But now they were telling her she would have to do it with anybody, at any given time. She didn't have a clue as to what she was supposed to do, but she was surrounded by young women who did, and they taught her what she needed to know.

She'll never forget her fear that first time. Until the last moment, she hoped somehow she would be able to get out of doing this. But that night, the *mamasan* told her to go sit with a customer who wanted to buy her a drink. This is usually a prelude to what follows. A client chooses a girl, buys a drink for her, and then determines if he wants to go further. If he does, he pays a "bar fine" – a set fee for taking the girl off the premises of the bar. The girl doesn't receive anything from the bar fee – but rather expects to get a tip after she performs the expected services.

Until the last moment, she hoped somehow she would be able to get away from doing this.

When a young woman goes off with the man, she never knows what she is getting into, unless he's a repeat customer. He may be kind and generous or he may be brutal – and he may send her off afterwards without a cent. She is at risk of being beaten and severely physically abused. On some occasions, there are other men in the room waiting for her and she is gang-raped. There is little protection for the women.

116

Just as Koy feared, after a short while the *farang* and the *mamasan* exchanged words and he paid the bar fine. The language barrier kept Koy and the man from even speaking to each other, but as she left the bar with the stranger and walked into this unknown, fearful scenario, she smiled and acted confident. Yet deep inside she screamed, "I don't want to! I don't want to do this!" Sadly, however, she felt she had no choice. She needed the money.

"Make sure he uses condoms!" were the last words of advice she received from the others as she left. Even the thought of asking this strange man to do that terrified her. But he agreed. It all seemed surreal to Koy, and when their time was over, she simply felt stunned. She had actually gone through with it. Now all Koy wanted to do was to get out of there as soon as possible!

But she had crossed the threshold – and like so many other girls, she began to work night after night. Koy was terrified at the beginning. Most of the clients at the bar were Americans and Europeans, so there was seldom any kind of verbal communication. She was simply expected to perform the required services.

Of course, Koy, like almost every other girl who works the bars, had a hope, a dream, that she clung to – that one of the *farangs* who came along would fall in love with her and rescue her from this life. But it seldom works out that way. Even though there actually are cases in which a Western client decides to set up housekeeping with one of the girls, it usually doesn't last very long. After a while, the man moves on, leaving his "girl" brokenhearted and sometimes even with a child or two. In that case, the father may send money for a while, but that rarely lasts long. So she ends up once again in the bar scene.

§

Koy worked the bars for five years and it never did get easier. She drank heavily to ease the pain and shame, and then she began taking drugs. Even though she worked hard, she didn't see her life getting any better. It felt like she was in the middle of a never-ending, raging storm. Yes, she made money every night, but then she used it up partying and gambling, so it would be gone by the next evening.

And then, one of her customers got her pregnant. Obviously, working the bars was no longer an option. She soon ran out of money and couldn't find any other kind of work. With one child already and another coming along, all doors slammed shut on her. "You need to go back home to your village," they told her. But how could she? She didn't want to go back and embarrass her parents. They didn't know the kind of work she was involved in. She was afraid of what their reaction would be. She felt so bad and ashamed!

When the *mamasan* realized the situation, she kindly took Koy under her wing, allowing her to stay with her. Then one night, she came back from work and told Koy, "Annie's team was at the bar tonight. I told them about your situation. They are willing to help you if you will allow them to. I can take you to where they are."

Koy knew who she was talking about. Annie headed a group of very kind women called NightLight. They would come into the bars several times a week and talk to the girls. They talked about God's love and offered them help to get out of this lifestyle. Koy had never spoken to these women personally, but she knew of other girls who had.

Koy realized that these women were probably the only ones who could help her at this point, so she and the *mamasan* went to NightLight's headquarters. Koy was awed by the genuine concern these women showed her. She hadn't even seen a doctor for prenatal treatment yet, so they registered her at a hospital. A few days afterward, it was Koy's birthday – but she didn't have a penny to her name. One of Annie's staff called her in, "I have a birthday gift for you," she said and handed her a card with money. Koy couldn't believe it. "But, where did this come from?" she asked. The woman smiled, "This gift came to you from a foreigner who cares about you and your wellbeing."

How was this possible? Koy wondered. All of her life, Koy had toiled to receive every single cent she had ever earned. Before working the bars, the money had been barely enough to get by. After performing humiliating services while working at the bars, the men sometimes sent her away without paying her anything, or gave her so little it just reinforced the feelings of low self-worth. Yet now, for the first time ever, she had received a gift – from someone she didn't even know. What kind of love was this?

What kind of love was this?

Nevertheless, it took some time before Koy was ready to accept the invitation to receive Christ. Hearing that there was a God who cared for her personally was new to her. All of Koy's life she had been used and abused. She felt there was no one who would ever care for her or help her. Why should she believe everything could be different? But the staff's kindness and unconditional love began to slowly chisel away the hardness and mistrust that Koy had formed in her heart. Ten days after her arrival at NightLight, the dam finally crumbled and she ran into the arms of her loving, forgiving Savior.

Koy had a long journey ahead, but every step of the way they were with her. When it turned out that she had to have a C-section, there was miraculous provision for the surgery. When she saw her healthy newborn baby, all she could do was thank and praise God. Because of her lifestyle, and particularly because of all the alcohol she had consumed, she was terribly afraid that something would be wrong with the baby. But when she saw her face, her immediate reaction was, "She's so beautiful! Thank You, God!"

When Koy had first found out she was pregnant, she was filled with regret, thinking that having a baby would be just a tremendous burden at this time. Now she was filled with joy, seeing her baby Banyi as a precious gift from God. At the same time, as she experienced God's love toward her child, she came to a better understanding of God's love toward her. She could believe in and truly feel God's unconditional love and acceptance toward her. And she loved Him, oh, how she loved Him!

NightLight's staff worked with Koy to help her gradually find wholeness. Buddhism is deeply ingrained into almost all Thais, and it requires a lot of hard work to transform mindsets and shake off all the consequences. For one thing, Buddhism allows for many other "gods" or spirits, so an important step for someone who wants to convert to Jesus is understanding that He is not simply "another" god to fill in the gaps, but the ONE and ONLY God. He will supply everything, but demands exclusive honor and worship.

Buddhism also teaches that women are less than men, going so far as to say that they were born women because of sin in a past life. They must do good deeds in order to reach another level and be born male in their next life. The most common "good deed" for a poor, young village woman is to support her family financially, which too often requires submitting herself to sexual humiliation and degradation night after night. Many bars and other sexually-oriented businesses have shrines to Buddha and other spirits. The bar owners perform certain rites every night so that they will have good business.

When they realize how much God loves them – how much dignitity they have in Him – It is a delightful shock!

So when the young women come out of this life and realize how much God loves them – how much dignity they have in Him – it is a delightful shock! Of course, most of them have to go through personal deliverance and ministry to break off the curses and be healed from the past.

Every day Koy grew in the Lord, rejoicing in Him. There was so much peace! So many new friends who genuinely cared for her! She became a true worshipper in spirit and in truth. She began seeking out other bargirls, sharing with them about the changes in her life since she had come to Christ. Many of the girls she spoke to did then go to NightLight to hear about this loving Christ.

She was now given an honorable way to make a living. NightLight supports the women who come for help by teaching them how to make high-end jewelry, which they then sell.

Still, there remained an area of sadness in Koy's life. When she had plunged into prostitution, she felt so ashamed that she cut off all ties with her family, including her first child. The last time she had seen them she had simply told them that she worked in a restaurant as a server. This is the paradox these beautiful women have to live with daily. On the one hand, they believe they are doing a good deed by earning money for their families. But, if they are doing "good deeds," then why do they hate it so much? Why are they filled with such feelings of shame to the degree that they do not want to admit to their own parents what they are doing to support them?

People kept asking her if she was going home to see her family. But for her, facing them again seemed like an enormous mountain, impossible to overcome. She began to pray that God would help her so that one day she would feel ready to go home. She had been a Christian for two years when God answered in a totally unexpected way: her sister actually called her! "Koy," she asked, "why don't you come home?" Koy was speechless, but her sister insisted. "Don't you miss your child?" (referring to her firstborn). "Of course I do," Koy answered, "but I don't have any money right now to go home."

At her sister's insistence, Koy finally stirred up enough courage to call her father. He seemed so happy to hear her voice! And then, he too asked when she was coming home. When she explained that she couldn't afford to, he told her that he would send her brother to get her.

When Koy saw all that her father was willing to do in order for her to go home, she felt special, and realized he really did miss her. About a week later her brother came for her. Her parents seemed glad to see her and their little granddaughter. They didn't ask her any questions about what she had been involved in, but she perceived that they knew. They seemed genuinely concerned and simply said, "You've been through some really difficult times, haven't you?"

The biggest surprise, however, was her stepmother's response to her - it was drastically different. Koy had always dreaded going back to the village because in the past her stepmother pressured her about money. Whenever she went home, her stepmother compared her to other village girls, telling Koy that they were better daughters because they sent more money home. She particularly did this if Koy came back home without extra money to leave with them. This only reinforced Koy's feelings of rejection – that her stepmother didn't love her and saw her only as a means of support. Koy always left the village feeling bad – about herself and her stepmother.

But this time it was totally different. She told her that her baby was cute and how proud she was that Koy was taking good care of her daughter. She didn't ask her who Banyi's father was or anything else that would make Koy ashamed. She simply encouraged Koy in all the good decisions she was making. For the first time ever, Koy felt like her stepmother loved her! A great healing took place in Koy's heart. God had answered her prayers. He had not only changed her, but her stepmother, too!

Koy continues to live in Bangkok with her little girl, working as a jewelry designer with NightLight. Often she leads worship during their devotional times. She says: "I think it is a gift that God has given me to serve Him. I love worshipping God. He has me serve Him through the gifts He has given me – and He has given me the gift of worship." Jesus gave Koy beauty for her ashes and joy for her mourning. *For it was for Koy's tears that Jesus died.*

This story is based on a personal account given by Koy to Carol Martinez and Malina Zlatkova. For more information about NightLight and how you can become involved, visit nightlightinternational.com.

Straightening up, Jesus said to her, "Woman, where are they? Did no one condemn you?"

She said, "No one, Lord."

And Jesus said, "I do not condemn you, either. Go from now on and sin no more."

John 8:10-11

RESCUED FROM SHAME

Fon's Story

*F*on was born in the village of Trat, Thailand. Fon's father had two wives, and there was no question about which he loved more: The second wife and her children. In fact, it appeared to Fon that they were the only family her father loved! Fon was the first wife's daughter, and grew up watching her father give attention and love to the other family while she was neglected. Instead of love and affirmation, whenever anything went wrong in the family, the first wife's family always got the blame and was punished for it. Far from feeling loved and protected by her father, she was terrified of him. He only inspired fear and she didn't even want to be near him. As she grew up, never once did he give her any hope that he loved her – even a little bit.

On the other hand, she knew her mother loved her, but undoubtedly she took out the stress of her husband's rejection on her own children. Instead of showing Fon love, she was always scolding and yelling at her. There were times when Fon wondered if she really was their daughter because they couldn't even tell her when her birthday was.

Fon grew up feeling like she didn't have any hope in her life. She didn't even want to be close to people, and things were about to get even worse. When she was 19, a man she had met through a mutual friend raped her. In Thailand, when a young woman is raped, people don't show compassion to her because she brings stigma and shame on the family. So Fon, rather than seeking help and justice, kept the rape to herself and was filled with shame. "Why am I even alive?" she asked herself. Finally, she thought she had found the easy way out – she took an overdose of pills, trying to kill herself. She lived, but the baby she had inside her, a product of the rape, died. By then, her family and all of the villagers were aware of what had happened. Of course, instead of support and understanding, she became the subject of village gossip. Life was then even more unbearable.

Finally, she thought she had found another way out – someone asked her to marry him. She didn't love him, but she saw him as her ticket to get away from her family and move somewhere else, so she married him. He almost immediately began to mistreat her. She had two children with him but, as Fon shares, "The longer we were married, the more he drank, the more fights we had over just about anything, and the more I hated him."

Then he began to gamble. When he was not out gambling and drinking with his friends, he was at home sleeping. If he made any money, Fon and their two boys never benefited from it. Fon had to work hard at a semi-precious stone farm to support herself and her family, sometimes not getting home until 1:00 A.M. or even later. She knew that she would have to get up in just a few hours to take care of her children and then go back to work. But often when she did come home, exhausted, her husband was waiting for her and would force her to have sex with him. When she tried to avoid sleeping with him, he humiliated her and beat her up. He was always accusing her of sleeping with other men and beat her for that, too. When she had an accident and broke her collarbone, instead of helping her, or even feeling sorry for her, he demanded that she have sex with him. Fon lived with him that way for ten years, but every day she hated him more. All she could think during those final years was that she wanted to kill him.

Fon realized that she needed to leave him as soon as possible, "Because soon either he will kill me or I will kill him," she thought.

One night her smallest boy became very sick and she wanted to take him to the hospital. When she asked her husband to go with her, his temper flared and he began to beat her – so badly that she was bleeding. Her sick child ran to her, trying to protect her, but he just kept on beating her, bypassing the child. By then Fon realized that she needed to leave him as soon as possible because, "Soon either he will kill me or I will kill him," she thought.

She knew that in order to leave she would literally have to escape. So finally she left, taking her smallest son. She made the difficult decision of leaving her oldest son with her husband because she knew there was no way she would be able to get away with both of them. With a broken heart, she left him there, but cried and cried, thinking about him all the time.

She went to another town and began looking for a job. The only job she could find was working with someone who made hair beads. Even though her little boy went to kindergarten in the morning, afterward he stayed with her late into the evening while she worked. Her boss didn't like this and Fon did everything she possibly could to make sure her little boy wouldn't upset him, even hitting the child to keep him quiet. Fon shares, "Sometimes my boss would buy chicken wings and feed them to his dog in front of my child. My child would have loved to eat some of those wings. They were a luxury I couldn't afford. But the owner would never give him any."

Finally, Fon realized she had no alternative other than to take her little boy back to the village and ask her sister to take care of him. But when she returned to the other town, no one would give her a job. Then she met someone who told her, "Go and work in Pattaya. The money is good." Fon's immediate reaction was "Never!" She knew well what kind of jobs there were in Pattaya and it brought back the memories of the rape and sexual abuse by her husband. She would never get involved in the sex industry!

But she had reached the end of her rope. She had left the only two people she felt loved her in the hands of others, because she couldn't care for them. She felt her life had no value anymore. Then she heard that her family back home was beating her little boy every night because he cried for her. She reasoned that if she sent more money home, they would treat her children better. If she had more money, she would have more power over the circumstances.

So she decided to go to Pattaya after all. She said to herself, "Just do it! It's for my children and if I die, I die!"

§

She started working at one of Pattaya's infamous "bars." At first she tried to avoid sleeping with customers by doing all of the dishwashing. She would wear clothes that totally covered her body, and then she sat in the back where no one would see her. But one day the manager told her, "It's time for you to come up to the front. If you want to keep your job, you must wear fewer clothes and start revealing your body. You need to wear high heels and talk with the customers." She recognized that her time had come for what she dreaded the most. If she refused to get involved with the men, she would lose her job. It was the only way to survive.

What kind of life was this? Everyday she doubted that life was worth living. The only thing that kept her going was the thought of her two sons.

Earning money this way was practically unbearable. She shares, "If I hadn't gotten drunk every night, I would not have been able to go through with it. So I would just get so drunk that I didn't know what was going on. Only then could I do what the men wanted me to do, but inside I was in a lot of pain. During the day I didn't want to go anywhere because I felt so much shame. I was afraid that during the day I would run into men that I had been with at night."

Fon began to drink all the time, drinking and drinking, to the point of throwing up. What kind of life was this? Every day she doubted if life was worth living. The only thing that kept her going was the thought of her two sons.

§

One evening several women came into the bar where she was working and struck up a conversation with her. They told her they were from Tamar Center, a place where she could take free English classes. They also invited her to a special party. All of this seemed very odd to Fon. What was the catch? Nevertheless, she decided to go to the party. It would be a break from her usual routine. Once there, she was intrigued with everything. "What is going on here?" she asked herself. "They are showing so much love and seem so genuinely concerned about me!"

Fon shares:

"For the first time in my life I started talking to God and I felt like He was really there. Until then, I had no hope."

And then she heard them say, "If you do something wrong, God can forgive you." Fon thought about that, realizing that was exactly what she needed. But she still couldn't see any reason to fully trust them. Why did they claim they loved her? And who was this Son of God they talked about so much?

For Fon, that party was a special break in her usual life, but she wasn't ready to trust the kind women who offered her and the rest of the bargirls a better life. So the next night, she was back on the job, hating it, and drinking as much as she possibly could to block the feelings without totally blacking out.

One day, though, she drank so much that she got terribly sick and began throwing up. While she retched, the images of all of the men who came and paid a price to use and abuse her came to her mind. She felt so much hatred toward herself for everything she did with them and for the drinking in order to do it. Suddenly, she cried out, "God, You know I don't want to drink like this - but they represent all my tears."

She shares: "For the first time in my life I started to talk to God, and I felt like He was actually there. I sensed that He was really listening to me and understood all the pain I was going through. Up until then I had no hope."

All of the men she had been with came to her mind and she thought, "When they wanted something from me, they actually acted like they loved me, but when they were through with me, they would treat me like garbage!" One recent client who had promised her so much had even convinced her to stay with him for 15 days. Then he betrayed her, leaving her without paying her anything!

Fon was also pained because her family back home didn't know what kind of work she was in. Her son would be so ashamed of her if he found out! And, of course, there was always the fear of contracting AIDs. Even though they were instructed to use condoms, nothing was 100 percent sure.

"I was so disappointed in my life! And so ashamed! I didn't know where to turn - where to go." She recognized she didn't even have any true friends, since the bargirls she was with weren't loyal to one another, either. They stole each other's belongings and were quick to blame others for it. Often, she was falsely accused of this.

Overwhelmed by her feelings of pain, shame and hopelessness, she went out to walk on the beach in the pre-dawn hours. It was still dark, but she didn't care. She walked for hours, processing her situation. She kept thinking, "I've totally lost my mind. If anyone wants to kill me while I'm out walking here alone, let them do it!" Then a *farang* (foreigner) tried to approach her. It was the last thing she wanted at this moment! So she started to run to get away from him. To her dismay, he started running after her! "He's chasing me as if I were a dog!" she thought. "I'm tired of this! I want to go where nothing is happening! I don't want to fight anymore!"

"As soon as I got there, I felt embraced by love."

At that moment, she saw only one way out – she would throw herself into the ocean. As she started walking into the water, she heard a voice that said, "Stop! Stop hurting yourself!"

To this day she doesn't know where the voice came from, but it made her stop. Suddenly, the kind women from Tamar Center came to her mind. They had given her their phone number and had told her she could call them whenever she wanted. Seeing them as her only lifeline at this critical moment, she immediately called them, but no one answered. She called them several times more, with the same result. Desperate, she called out: "God, if someone doesn't pick up the phone this time, I'll kill myself!"

This time someone did answer, and listened as Fon poured out her feelings of despair. The first words from the woman on the other end of the line were "God loves you." Those words touched

Fon's heart. Even so, she still asked herself, "Is there really anyone who loves me?" She had to find out! So she accepted the invitation to go to Tamar Center.

"As soon as I got there, I felt embraced by love. They told me Jesus promised, 'Come to Me, all who are weary and heavy-laden, and I will give you rest' (Matthew 11:28). Oh, how I needed rest!" Fon also experienced an amazing miracle the very first day she went. She had tried time and again to stop drinking, but it was impossible. That first day at Tamar Center, she called out, saying, "God, I don't want to drink anymore," and she never drank again!

§

The women there began to help her. Every day they patiently studied the Bible with her until she realized she could trust their love – and even more so, God's. She felt like she was finally finding peace, and she invited Jesus to come into her life. As she embraced God's love, she realized that to be truly free from all the oppression of the past, she would have to get rid of all her idols.

"Jesus took all my shame away. Through His love, I now have value and strength and want to share His love with everyone."

She obeyed God and got rid of all her idols. But she continued to feel oppression. Meanwhile, at home a mirror kept falling. She would pick it up and put it in its place, but shortly after, it would be on the floor again. This seemed strange to her until one day when she was in the room when it fell again. At that moment, a little drawer in the mirror spilled open and a tiny idol she had totally forgotten about appeared to literally jump out of the drawer! She immediately took it to Tamar Center where they burned it in a special place where they had burned many other idols. After that, all the oppression left.

Miracles also began to take place in her family. Her oldest son, now 17, was violent, full of anger and hatred after living for years with his physically abusive father who beat him constantly. Fon started to pray for her children every day, but the more she cried out to God, the worse her son became. Finally, a miracle happened and he, too, accepted Christ. He has become a young man on fire for God. Everyone is shocked at the transformation in this young man who shares God's love wherever he goes. He is now making excellent grades in school and wants to go to the discipleship training school. Her 11-year-old son, who now lives with her in Pattaya, is also doing very well.

This has been a great witness to her family, who thought she had lost her mind when she accepted Christ. They are the first to admit that the change in her children is a miracle they thought impossible. This opened the door for them, too, to gradually open their hearts to God. The father she feared so much has since passed away, but she was first able to totally reconcile with him and even hug him, letting him know that she loved him.

Now, when Fon goes to the village to see her family, the villagers say, "Jesus has come to the village!"

And indeed, He has. Fon says, "Jesus took all my shame away. Through His love, I now have value and strength and want to share His love with everyone."

Fon now works at Tamar Center. As she trains new arrivals to make rice paper greeting cards – one of the ways the women support themselves – she encourages them to also fully trust God. Fon is truly a light that shines! **It is for her tears – and the tears of so many other women who feel forced into this degrading lifestyle, that Jesus Died.**

This chapter is based on a personal account, given by Fon, of Tamar Center, Pattaya, Thailand, to Carol Martinez and Malina Zlatkova. To learn more about Tamar Center and how you can become involved, go to ywamthai.org/pattaya/tamar_update.html.

He lifted me out of the slimy pit,

out of the mud and mire;

he set my feet on a rock

and gave me a firm place to stand.

He put a new song in my mouth,

a hymn of praise to our God.

Many will see and fear

and put their trust in the Lord.

Psalm 40:2-3 (NIV)

AMAZING GRACE
THE SPIRITUAL JOURNEY OF A LADYBOY

Miaow's Story

Miaow was different from most of the little boys in the Bangkok neighborhood where he grew up. He didn't enjoy boy games but preferred to play with the girls. By the time he was seven, he actually felt like he was a little girl. This didn't bother his parents at all. In Thailand, "transgenderism" is accepted by many, to the point of calling "ladyboys" the third sex. Often, when parents think they see this tendency in a son, they go so far as to provide them with female hormones and other means of developing their femininity. Up until early 2008, it was even legal to castrate underage boys. Thankfully, this didn't happen to Miaow.

Miaow's parents, instead of being concerned or ashamed, actually applauded him. His mother dressed him up in skirts and blouses. "You are so lovely – just like a little girl!" they'd tell him, smiling approvingly and showing him off to others. Miaow continued to grow up, certain that being a ladyboy for the rest of his life was his destiny. He was very intelligent and loved to study. At 17, he had finished high school with honors and was studying at the university.

But then, something happened. His parents totally turned against his lifestyle and became ashamed of him. Miaow never understood why the sudden change. Perhaps it was because they wanted a better future for their son. Even though ladyboys are "culturally accepted," the truth is that they face many limitations. Few people take them seriously and it would be difficult for Miaow to be accepted in the professional world. Many Buddhists believe that being a ladyboy is a consequence of bad karma or sin in a former life. Ladyboys are still subject to scorn by their peers and others. This is something no parents want for their children – and Miaow was their only child. So they began to continuously berate him. "It's time to start acting and dressing like the man you are!" they would tell him.

The problem was that by then Miaow didn't have the slightest notion of how to "be a man." During all of his childhood he had been affirmed, loved, and accepted by those closest to him as a female. The loud arguments in his home continued until his parents gave him an ultimatum. If he didn't change, he would no longer be accepted in their home. Filled with pain, confusion, and anger from being totally rejected by his parents, he walked out and moved in with friends.

Miaow had a lot of friends and began to drown his pain in drinking and partying – especially at gay bars. Unlike his parents, his friends thought he was delightful and lots of fun, so he took comfort in his popularity. But he was not happy. All he really wanted to do every night was to get drunk and forget it all. Within a short time he was introduced to marijuana, then heroin. All of this was his attempt to drown away the pain and the sense of loss he felt.

During all his childhood he had been affirmed, loved and accepted by those closest to him as a female.

His dreams of finishing school shattered and, needing money to help him pay for his new habits, everything went in a downward spiral. He had run out of money and knew he couldn't go back home. The truth was that now there was no turning back. He was taking female hormones, so his breasts developed, his voice changed, and he began to take on more and more female characteristics. A number of his ladyboy friends were selling their bodies for sex and they began convincing him it would be the only way he would be able to support himself. Even so, it was a hard pill to swallow.

Miaow knew he wouldn't have any trouble turning tricks. He was very attractive and there had already been a number of *farangs* (foreigners) who tried to persuade him to go with them. But it was so degrading for this former university student who had dreamed of pursuing a professional career! Finally, without money, he felt he had no other choice. He went to a discotheque with a friend, and there he accepted his first customer, a German tourist. Miaow was still just 17 at the time.

Miaow shares, "At first, it was really bad – both painful and degrading – for me. But after a while I became accustomed to it because I did it every day, often several times a night. Sometimes the men became very sadistic and they would beat me or hurt me in other ways. I was forced to engage in every depraved act imaginable. But I felt I had no choice because I had no money. It became a way of life."

It became such a way of life that he went a step further in denying his sexual identity. He moved to Pattaya, a beach town known for it sex tourism, and totally took on the identity of a woman. Few people knew the truth. He had long, beautiful hair and, thanks to the hormones, a very developed "female" body. He never had any surgeries, but he became adept at hiding his male anatomy. Having the appearance of a beautiful young woman, he then left the gay bar scene and applied at a regular discotheque which hired only females. The owner didn't have a clue, and Miaow began a new career as a female go-go dancer. He danced well and became very popular – foreign straight men would flock to see this beautiful "woman." Eventually he even caught the eye of the local newspaper. His picture appeared in it, recognizing him as the best go-go dancer in all of Pattaya.

Everyone thought he was a woman. He was even able to fool the very drunk foreign men he had sex with late at night. When his boss finally learned that Miaow was a man, he was surprised, but told Miaow to continue with the farce because he was very popular and making a lot of money for the bar.

Miaow tried to convince himself he was happy; maybe his parents had rejected him, but here everyone loved him. He was making more money than he could ever imagine. He would often see six or more customers per night. Then he would sleep all day and not get up until late in the afternoon, only to start working again at 8:00 in the evening. Because he catered to foreign men, he studied English and was proud of his handle of the language. But the truth was that by then he was an alcoholic and totally dependent on amphetamines and heroin. Then there was always the threat of STDs and that very dreaded disease...

One day Miaow decided it would be a good idea to have a check-up. He felt fine, but he thought there would be no harm in having one. When he asked the doctor for a blood test, the practitioner looked him straight in the eye and asked him: "Are you sure you want to know?" Miaow, without skipping a beat, responded "yes."

A few days later the doctor called him in and gave him the news – he was HIV positive. Miaow was shocked! It couldn't be possible. He had always been careful! Besides, he didn't have any symptoms. Surely they had made a mistake. In total denial, he moved to Ko Chang Island, a popular getaway. He continued prostituting his body, even putting his customers at risk.

After a short time in Ko Chang Island, he began to develop a blistery rash – even so, he continued in denial. "They're just infected mosquito bites," he reasoned – though he was well aware that this was one of the most common symptoms of an HIV infection. But he believed he was indestructible! Then he found out that one of his closest friends was very sick from AIDS, so he went back to Pattaya to visit him. While there, the disease finally ravaged Miaow, too, landing him in the hospital.

As he lay in bed, weak and wracked with pain, he felt totally alone. Few people came to see him. Then one day, as he dozed in and out of consciousness, he heard a sweet voice singing. It was a melody about love – God's love. He opened his eyes and there he saw a tiny, partially blind woman looking at him. She smiled, introduced herself, and told him, "God loves you – He really does." She continued visiting him at the hospital and they became friends. He learned that this amazing woman, Pornsawan, also had HIV, only she hadn't acquired it as a prostitute – it had most likely come from an infected needle while receiving medical treatments. Many years before, she had been given three months to live. Funeral arrangements had already been made – when she was miraculously healed. At that time, she had made a commitment to God – if He allowed her to live, she would spend her life serving those with AIDS and other serious diseases.

...He heard a sweet voice singing. It was a melody about love – God's love.

Pornsawan was so different! Miaow was full of anger and bitterness, yet even though terrible things had happened to Pornsawan, she was full of love. What was it about her? He really liked talking with this woman!

Miaow eventually got better from his outbreak and was released from the hospital. When Pornsawan invited him to the small church she had started and now pastored, he accepted. This wasn't the first time Miaow had heard about God. In fact, even though his parents were Buddhist, they had sent him to a Catholic high school. He had studied the Bible on his own and had even recognized Jesus as the Son of God. But when he left home and embraced his lifestyle, all of that was conveniently forgotten. Even so, he never stopped recognizing the existence of God.

In this small church, however, he became reacquainted with the Lord – he realized that God loved him and had very special plans for him, if he would allow God to do a work in him. On

October 31, 2006, Miaow gave his heart to Jesus. "You must help me, Jesus!" he cried out. "I will abandon drugs and my lifestyle, but you must help me!"

Jesus did help, and Miaow made a commitment to no longer engage in sexual practices. It was hard for him because he was living with friends from his former lifestyle. But then Pornsawan invited him to live at the church. What a blessing! He now had plenty of time, so he spent hours every day studying his Bible, learning about God's everlasting love and His plan and promises for Miaow. Two Bible verses particularly impacted him.

He realized that God loved him and had very special plans for him.

One was, "There is neither Jew nor Greek, slave nor free, male nor female, for you are all one in Christ Jesus" (Galatians 3:28 NIV). When he read it, he felt like jumping up and down! "I'm included! I'm included!" he realized. Even though Miaow had totally sanctified his body before the Lord and was now keeping himself sexually pure, he still felt like a ladyboy. The many years of female hormones, living, thinking, and acting like a woman had taken its toll on him. Accepting Christ didn't mean that he would immediately grow a beard and speak with a deep voice, or feel comfortable in men's clothing. But here he understood that God would meet him where he was at that point in his life, then lovingly lead him to wholeness.

The other verse that impacted him was, "I can do all things through Him who strengthens me," (Philippians 4:13). Miaow cried out to God, "I don't want to be a ladyboy anymore, but I can't change on my own. You will have to help me change."

Miaow continues on that path to total wholeness. If you meet Miaow today, you may be surprised when you realize he is actually male. In many ways he still talks, walks, and acts like a woman. But hopefully you will get past that quickly and see him for what he really is – a child of God on fire for his Savior!

Miaow has totally given his life over to serving God and sharing and showing God's love to others. He visits HIV patients in the hospital and reads them the Bible. He prays with them as they lie on their deathbeds. He outright tells them they must surrender to God. He has seen many people get saved. Some people refuse to listen, but that doesn't stop him from witnessing every opportunity he finds. He says, "Every day we must testify. Everywhere I go I lead people to surrender to God, because only God can help them. Most people, once they get HIV, lose most of their friends. I lead them to a true friend, Jesus."

"Most people, once they get HIV, lose most of their friends. I lead them to a true friend, Jesus."

As he ministers, he has seen God work amazing miracles through him. He shares, "I had a friend who was dying and I told her, 'You must believe in Jesus. You must receive Jesus in your heart so you will meet Him when you die.' She did – and was healed! On another occasion, we witnessed to a woman who couldn't see. We prayed for her, and by the afternoon she could see again! Then she received Jesus in her heart." These are just two of the miracles he has seen.

Now, he serves full time at the hospice Pornsawan opened for HIV and TB patients – a facility on the outskirts of Pattaya with few material resources and little funding, but soaked in worship and the Word. When Pornsawan invited Miaow to work there, she told him she didn't have any money to pay him a salary. Nevertheless, every day they have food on the table. Says Miaow, "When Pornsawan invited me to come work for free, I told God my life belonged to Him. I had nothing at the time, not even a change of clothes. But since then God has given me everything. I am so happy to live here and sacrifice myself to God!"

Miaow looks after the patients, teaching them how to take their medicine and care for themselves. He gives them physical rehabilitation and spiritual counseling. He says, "I teach them about God and they are now all Christians. I don't know if they will die today or tomorrow, but when they do, they will now go to the Lord."

God has restored another dream for Miaow. He has gone back to the university and received his degree as a public health attendant, graduating with honors. When Pornsawan encouraged Miaow to go back to school, his first reaction was, "I'm over forty years old! What place do I have in school?" But when he looked through the prospectus and saw a career in public health, specifically geared toward dealing with patients in HIV, he immediately recognized it was God calling him to do it.

He has since set up an HIV clinic at a public hospital where several times a month he sees HIV patients and gives them counseling. Many patients arrive at the hospital for their first visit still in shock over the onset of the disease and without a clue as to what to do next. Miaow helps them to register and get ID cards. He sends them to the appropriate clinics and doctors, and also helps them get free medicine.

Miaow's heart now is to help ladyboys come to know God's love and to realize that through Him, they can live a pure life. At the HIV hospice there is another ladyboy, a young teen named Tip.

Miaow's heart now is to help ladyboys come to know God's love and to realize that through Him, they can live a pure life.

When Tip realized that Miaow was also a ladyboy, he asked Miaow how he was able to stop sleeping with men and quit smoking. Miaow explained to Tip that he could only do it through the Holy Spirit's power, after receiving Christ. Tip has now also accepted Christ. Miaow hopes that soon he can be involved in a ministry focused on witnessing to ladyboys in the bars.

There was another area in his life that Miaow realized he needed to resolve. When he opened his Bible to the Ten Commandments, every time he read, "Honor your father and your mother," he felt convicted. Other than trying to have a brief communication a few years earlier, he had severed all ties with his parents since the day he had left home at the age of 17. He began to pray about ways he could bridge the gap again. Even though he felt unsure about how his parents would receive him personally just yet, he knew it was very important that his parents come to know the Gospel. Through contacts he was able to make, he arranged for a pastor to witness to his parents – and both of them received Christ! His mother died shortly after and he has no doubt where she is now. His father is elderly, but Miaow goes and visits him and helps any way he can.

Sometimes Miaow encounters ladyboys and gay prostitutes that he knew in his former life, who are now also dealing with AIDS. They are always surprised to see him. He shares with them how God has changed his life. Says Miaow, "It's very difficult for ladyboys to change their lifestyles and many ask how I have been able to change."

Undoubtedly, Miaow is an example of redemption and transformation. He has probably done more in his few years as a Christian than most do in a lifetime! His HIV is in remission and he enjoys good health. However, he is the first to say he feels like there is still "unfinished business"in his life. He shares, "I still feel like a woman, and I know that is not good for me. However, my body can't change from one moment to another on its own. I know that one day God can change my appearance and heart. I feel sad because there are many Christian people who have outright said to me, 'How can you be a Christian? Ladyboys are bad!' My answer is that all I know is that I love God. I have abandoned all the bad things I did. I am not engaging in sexual experiences anymore – I am living a totally pure sexual lifestyle. Even if I am a ladyboy, I really believe God doesn't judge my appearance but my heart, and is pleased with what I do now! And I know, I can do all things through Christ who strengthens me!"

Yes, surely God is pleased with Miaow. As he visits HIV patients in the hospital and hospice, ministering salvation and miracles of healing, he is a trophy of God's grace. **It is for Miaow's tears – and those of the thousands of young men like him – that Jesus died!**

This chapter is based on Miaow's personal testimony, as told to Carol Martinez and Malina Zlatkova.

PART FOUR:

Love War
Reports from Soldiers on the Front Lines

The stories in this final section are from those who, like Jesus, saw the multitude and were "moved with compassion" (Matthew 9:36 KJV). This compassion has led to action that is making a difference for Jesus' sake.

"When I visited Poipet (Cambodia), I saw a lot of children crossing the border into Thailand. These children had to work and couldn't go to school. Crossing the border illegally, they were chased by the police who would beat them and then put them in an open jail cell out in the sun for everyone to see. Other times I saw them crossing the border near dangerous land mines. I was greatly burdened and began to pray, "God, these people need someone to help them!" And God led me to quit my job and come here..."

Chomno, Cambodian Hope Organization

"You may choose to look the other way, but you can never say again that you did not know." — *William Wilberforce*

LOVE WAR
The Stories

He has showed you, O man,

what is good.

And what does the Lord require of you?

To act justly and to love mercy

and to walk humbly with your God.

Micah 6:8 (NIV)

LOVE THAT NEVER FAILS

Michele's Story

*I*t was a day that dawned like any other. The March 2009 morning quickly went from warm to hot, and the feel of a storm hung faintly in the air. Little did we know the storm that awaited us was more than the distant clouds gathering on the horizon foretold.

I had moved to this war-torn patch of earth in Southern Sudan in 2006 to pioneer Iris Ministries in the area, not too long after the peace agreement was signed, which ended Africa's longest running civil war. It has been a region plagued by instability, violence, and profound need. Here, one in two children die before they reach their fifth birthday. Medical care is almost nonexistent for most people, while 15 of the world's 16 deadliest diseases run rampant.

The year I moved here, Sudan had the dubious distinction of being dubbed the world's most failed state. I had asked God to send me to the worst place He would trust me with. In a way, it was kind of a compliment from heaven – a promotion if you will – to be trusted with a place most consider an enigma and where even many aid agencies have little expectation of lasting change.

In almost three years since opening our doors, Iris Ministries in Sudan had grown from a promise in my heart into 90 children calling me Mama at our main base. This also included works in three other regions, multiple churches, hundreds of children receiving education, and thousands being reached with the love and good news of Jesus. The Kingdom of God was breaking forth as the blind saw, the deaf heard, and many, many were set free from bondage to the enemy.

We had recently moved onto our new land a few miles from the southwestern commerce hub of Yei. It was forty acres of heaven for our children after two years of being cooped up on less than a dusty acre of rental property in the middle of town.

I woke up that morning with a sense of foreboding in my spirit. Quickly I dismissed it as the day brought with it its usual share of crises waiting to be resolved and babies waiting to be snuggled. It was nearing lunchtime when I noticed looks of concern silently being exchanged between our staff.

We live in a volatile area where stability is often a pleasant illusion. I went over to find out what the problem was that day. The radio had just reported that a band of the Lord's Resistance Army, a cultish rebel group known for their intense brutality, was less than ten miles away and headed in our direction. I looked up to see our children with their clothes packed and ready to run into the relative safety of town. Being on the outskirts of town would in the natural leave us vulnerable to attack. Concern was deeply etched on our senior leaders' faces. "Mama, this is not good," they said soberly.

One thing almost three years here had taught me was not to make decisions based on fear. We only move where we see God moving. The radio had the great propensity at times for sensationalism, so I sent several of our leaders into town to check out the real story. They returned confirming the radio reports. Where the LRA had been the night before, several were killed. Children were abducted. The clouds gathering on the horizon were not the only storm brewing in the early afternoon heat.

Our entire neighborhood had fled into town in fear of the terror that stalked in the night.

Around 3 P.M. we went into town briefly to check out the latest intelligence with other agencies and email a brief prayer request. The storm was gathering in intensity all around us. While we were gone, local officials had gone on the radio instructing everyone to pull out their machetes and AK-47s and be prepared to fight. Our choices were narrowing rapidly before our eyes.

The hallmark of the LRA is kidnapping children to be used as sex slaves, porters, and child soldiers, as well as the gruesome maiming of their victims and actions that are purely evil. Should we stay on our compound with 90 children and some older mamas, protected only by two guards armed with bows and arrows? Or should we evacuate into town and risk spending the night in the open with 90 kids and fearful mobs carrying automatic weapons and machetes? Not exactly a win-win situation in the natural! I am so happy we live beyond the seen in a supernatural reality.

On the way back to the compound, the road was hauntingly reminiscent of disaster movies I had seen, where everyone else is running in the opposite direction. Murmurs of, "Run, run, the LRA are coming!" rippled throughout the crowds, as fear hardened their expressions into focused stares in the fading evening light. Just as we turned off onto the dirt road leading to our compound, one lone motorbike screeched by with a woman shouting and swinging a machete over her head. Silently we bounced the rest of the way home.

I was greeted by everyone in our children's center anxiously awaiting the verdict. Should we stay or go? Our entire neighborhood had fled into town in fear of the terror that stalked in the night. The area was a virtual ghost town as we drove by.

I knew in my spirit we must stay. We drove onto our land and I saw angels in the spirit standing at attention all along our fence. No matter what it looked like, we would be safe here. God was in control. I heard very clearly the voice of my Jesus who is my everything, "Beloved, I don't want you to run, I want you to worship."

Now please understand that some of our children were former victims of the LRA. They knew the terror all too well. We were staking everything on God's Word by staying. It was not a light decision, but when God speaks, He speaks. It was not a light decision, but it was a simple one.

I got down from our truck and was thronged by children and staff wanting to know what we would do. We all sat down and I announced that we would not be running into town like everyone expected. Jesus had said to stay and worship. Questioning looks swept through the crowd. The light was quickly fading and the LRA was known to attack soon after nightfall.

With our staff we decided that all of the children and mamas would sleep together in three of the sturdiest houses that were made of cement with metal doors and windows. Our older boys and missionary staff would patrol the compound. After the arrangements were made, we gathered everyone in the courtyard and our older girls began to lead in worship. Soon the typical nightly love song to Jesus was rising with even greater fervor than normal. Some time into the worship, the beats of the bamboo sticks on our plastic jerrycans slowed, and one by one the children began dropping to their faces, weeping into the dirt. I leaned closer to listen to their prayers.

> To my astonishment, they were not crying out for our safety; they were crying out for the salvation of the LRA.

To my astonishment, they were not crying out for our safety; they were crying out for the salvation of the LRA!

"Jesus, please let the rebels know You. Let them know they are loved, not orphans, and they don't have to kill people. Show them your love and forgiveness."

Tears of gratitude streamed down my face. Into this storm, all heaven was invading through the prayers of our children. Holy Spirit hovered as a tangible weight in the atmosphere, pushing back the fear that had tried to seize our compound in its grips. As the children began to stand back up, I prayed for their eyes to be opened in the Spirit to what God was doing. I told them to look toward our fence and asked them what they saw.

"Mama, there are angels all along our fence." There sure were! I was encouraged that our children also saw them. We stood together and in one voice commanded the spirit of fear to get off our compound:

"Rohol al koff, ruwa bara be isiim tai Jesua." Spirit of fear, *get out in the name of Jesus.*

Then we loosed the angels assigned to protect us. We thanked Jesus in advance for His loving guard over all of us. I sent most of the younger children off to their houses to sleep while I sat up with some of our older youth who were joining the watchmen in patrolling in shifts. We talked through Psalm 91 and watched it come alive all during the night.

> "Mama, there are angels all along our fence." There sure were! I was encouraged that our children also saw them.

The next morning was Sunday. Did we have church! We were ALIVE! Shortly after a jubilant worship time together, stories from the night came trickling in. We had more reason to celebrate than we knew.

As the stories unfolded, we found out the LRA band of rebels were headed straight for us. They had massacred a family less than a mile from our compound. For some unknown reason, they stopped, turned around, and went the opposite direction. No one completely knows why. But we do! They saw our angels. That is my theory at least.

But the story actually only begins there. This just sets the stage for the real drama that would be played out. A few days later some frustrated aid workers appeared at my door. They recounted their struggles of trying to counsel a three-year-old little girl who was a victim in the attack. She was forced to watch her mother viciously murdered and then was clubbed in the head with rocks and left for dead. She had been unconscious for three days and recently came to. But she was catatonic and they were unsuccessful in "counseling" her.

I wondered how many non-traumatized three-year-olds they had "counseled" successfully. There are moments when God's compassion so grips your heart that it leaps out in front of all your common sense and you hear yourself speaking words you would not speak if you had thought them through in advance. I heard myself speaking to them, "Bring her here, I know how to help her." *Well, THAT was bold, Michele. Jesus, help! This had better be You or I am toast.*

I hopped in their vehicle and a few moments later was cradling three-year-old Charity close to my heart. I was holding "love" in my arms. She had a vacant stare into some distant nothingness and was totally unresponsive. Her skull was smashed in on one side from the bludgeoning she had received, and one-third of one side of her head was soft to the touch. This once vivacious little girl now could not walk without help, talk, or even feed herself.

> I was holding "love" in my arms.

I cannot even begin to describe to you the depths of compassion that welled up in my heart. As I held her, we arranged with the neighbors to have her, and two of her brothers, come and live with us. The eldest brother had been abducted by the rebels. Their single mother was horrifically murdered in front of them. It was nothing less than miraculous that these children were alive.

The next day, Charity and her remaining siblings moved in with us. She became my almost-constant companion for the next ten days. I sat with her and did the thing I knew to do – love her, sing over her and pray. Our staff and I were praying and caring for her 24/7 for the next week and a half. We did not have the answers in the natural. All we knew was His love was being poured out through our lives into her shattered frame.

We celebrated seemingly small gains, which often reverted into setbacks. But our eyes were not on Charity's brokenness; our eyes were fixed on His provision for her healing. Even so, we were researching ways to get her to neighboring countries for medical evaluation. Her skull was apparently fractured and partly squishy. This was not normal. Finally we had a breakthrough and funding was offered from an area agency. Still, we set our eyes in faith that God would do what no medical system could. He was healing her from the inside out. I knew it, even though every circumstance visibly defied that statement.

The day after receiving the news of the funding, her tenth day with us, I had run into town to do some shopping for a few hours. When I left Charity, she was sitting where she normally sat staring vacantly into space, her face utterly expressionless. When I returned, Charity was not sitting in her normal spot on her mat. I looked around to see what staff was helping her and where she was. I was concerned. Maybe she had wandered off.

Suddenly I heard high-pitched giggles behind me from some of our younger girls. I turned around to greet them and there was Charity, giggling and running with our other three- and four-year-old girls! I almost didn't believe my eyes. It was my turn to be speechless.

She noticed me standing there gaping at her and our eyes locked. I will never forget that moment. People want to know why I would leave suburban America for a war zone in Africa without running water or electricity, and why I would risk everything to follow the heart of my King. This is it. She ran - ran - to me and wrapped her delicate little arms around my waist. She looked up into my face with eyes shining and a smile that lit up her whole countenance as she confidently cried, "Mama!"

I was undone. Tears of joy began to stream down my face. I reached down to touch her small head and found the "squishy" spot had reduced from one-third of one side of her head to about the size of a U.S.A. dime. Over the next two days, it disappeared completely, and we began to get to know this beautiful miracle of His love, Charity, as the imaginative three-year-old princess she was.

> "We don't live in fear, we live in Jesus. He will care for us. We are not worried this time."

We then emailed the agency who had so graciously offered us funding for medical assistance. We thanked them but told them we no longer needed the money – Jesus had healed her! Charity's story made waves throughout their offices in our regional capital.

God is love that never fails. Before there ever was an LRA rebel movement, before Charity ever was conceived, Jesus saw the pain and the tears and the suffering, and He paid the price for her healing on the cross. There is nothing any of us has walked through in our lives that He has not already paid the price on the cross to heal. His love never fails. Charity is living proof.

But the story does not even end there. When God moves, He is building a living history that changes the way we see and interact with the world around us. We see His faithfulness in our past storms, so the next storm we encounter is simply another opportunity to watch Him move.

Six months later, the LRA again returned to less than ten miles from us. But this time it was a completely different story. Our staff and children were not even concerned. When our head mama was asked how she was doing given the situation, her reply was, "We don't live in fear, we live in Jesus. He will care for us. We are not worried this time."

> What GREAT love it takes to love and pray for an enemy that has raped and pillaged and stolen everything from you.

Unbeknownst to me, our children had decided enough was enough in the Spirit. They began to call for early morning prayer meetings in their houses. Getting up at 5 A.M., they worshipped and prayed, pouring their hearts out to Jesus, the altogether Faithful One.

They were tired of the enemy killing people in their backyard. They desired that the LRA would turn themselves in and then be able to go home and be reunited with their families. Our children were storming the gates of heaven that the captives in their midst might be set free. I was again undone by how Jesus was using these little lives laid down in love for Him and for their enemies.

I was reminded it takes no great love to love those who love you. BUT what GREAT love it takes to love and pray for an enemy that has raped and pillaged and stolen everything from you. Some of our children were praying not for an impersonal threat, but for the very enemy that had ripped apart their homes and lives. This was the miracle of the Gospel in action. This was the love of God that supernaturally transforms us from the inside out and covers a multitude of sins.

Three days later, all heaven began to join in God's response. A group of ten LRA walked into our police station of their own accord and turned themselves in. They said, "We are tired of killing people and stealing. Can you help us?" This does not happen in the natural. Not at all. But in the Kingdom of God, the prayers of the smallest child are enough to stop one of the most feared rebel movements on the planet.

This was supernatural. Where armies of the earth had failed, the prayers of children that know they are sons and daughters of their Papa in heaven were moving mountains! Our children were not crying out for vengeance or retribution, but for mercy on their enemies. How heaven must have marveled. Over the next six weeks, our children prayed each morning. Forty-seven more LRA rebels turned themselves in to our police headquarters. And just as our children prayed, many were able to be reunited with their families and be repatriated back to their communities.

Charity reminds me every day that the unfailing love of God is strong enough to look hate in the face and choose mercy – mercy that is powerful enough to cause rebels to bow their knees and even stop a war in its tracks. Her little life is my love letter from heaven.

Our weapons are not of this world, rather they are mighty for the destruction of strongholds and every lofty thing that exalts itself against the knowledge of Christ. Our battle, no matter how fierce, is never against flesh and blood. Our battle is in the Spirit.

Truly for their tears He died. For Charity's tears. But even for the tears of our most dreaded enemies. The greatest weapon there is, is His love. Those who wield His unfailing love are arising from the hidden depths of His heartbeat. Have you seen them? Have you seen the dangerous fearless lovers of our King, who has so captured their gazes, the storms around them are simply opportunities to dance on the waves in His embrace?

> He died even for the tears of our most dreaded enemies. The greatest weapon there is, is love.

They are the unlikely ones, the burning ones, the passionate ones the world has overlooked and called foolish. They will arise from the ends of the earth with a "Yes" cry in their hearts and a song sung with their lives. What would a people look like who are fully embraced by love? What would an army of love be? Sons and daughters released from the darkest corners of the earth to carry the light of His face reflected in their own, as they see who they really are in Love's eyes.

Little children, elderly mamas, local leaders, and missionaries from a world away all become one family dancing, spinning, finding who they are in His gaze. It is nothing less than supernatural and nothing other than Jesus bringing His Kingdom to those who know their need, to those who are willing to become humble like a little child, to those who are willing to pray for their enemies.

Together, we are learning to see our world through His eyes. Some of the most broken and feared will become the fearless lovers of His heart, the display of His beauty in the earth. Our hearts are overcome by a love we cannot contain. We only keep what we give away. So we will give to Him all we are - all our dreams, all our hopes, all our understanding, all our everything - until He takes our lives, holding them in the fire of His gaze, and we become the reflection of His glory in the earth.

Could an army be raised up to fight hate with love, injustice with mercy and truth, war with peace, poverty with generosity, despair with joy and praise, striving with rest, religion with freedom? We are watching the least and the unlikely arise with no desire but to capture Jesus' heart with the love song of their lives. And every day He is drawing us deeper into His unreasonable grace, His incomprehensible mercy, and His love that never fails.

This chapter is by Michele Perry, Field Ministry Director for Sudan for Iris Ministries, Inc. She lives in Southern Sudan and ministers around the world. Michele is also the founder of Converge International and the author of Love Has a Face: Mascara, a Machete and One Woman.

For more information and to learn how you can become involved, visit convergeinternational.net.

If I speak with the tongues of men and of angels, but do not have love, I have become a noisy gong or a clanging cymbal.

If I have the gift of prophecy, and know all mysteries and all knowledge; and if I have all faith, so as to remove mountains, but do not have love, I am nothing.

And if I give all my possessions to feed the poor, and if I surrender my body to be burned, but do not have love, it profits me nothing.

1 Corinthians 13:1-3

Sharing the Father's Love
on the Streets of Brazil
Nic's Story

Although Asia gets more press, according to many reports, Brazil has actually become the prostitution capital of the world, with approximately 1,500,000 men, women and children engaged in prostitution. Belem, a large city in Northern Brazil, was recently cited as the sexual paradise of the world by a major news magazine in Brazil. The saying for the city is, "You can get a girl of any age and whenever you want."

The root of the problem isn't prostitution itself but rather fatherlessness. We must address the heart of the issue, which is a lack of the realization that they have a Papa who loves them. We must stop attacking the surface conditions without touching the roots.

When we minister love to the root issue, we will have a great harvest of redeemed hearts.

A Broken Heart

My wife and I first went to Brazil about three years ago with Randy Clark of Global Awakening. Randy Clark is recognized for the signs and wonders that follow him, and it was exciting to be involved in his ministry. Under Randy's leadership, we were ministering in healing services in several churches, praying for the sick, casting out the demons and declaring freedom to the captives. During the whole trip there were miracles, signs and wonders every night – 400 were healed and about 200 received Jesus. I was asked to preach the very last night of the trip and I was excited! All I had to do was ride on Randy's coattails! I would stand at the pulpit, extend my hand, and simply say, "More, Lord!" and everyone would fall to the ground, many being healed and saved. The Lord would be glorified, and then we could all go out to eat.

So I didn't even bother to prepare – I had it all figured out. However, while riding the bus on the way to church that night, I realized it might be a good idea to check with the Lord to see if He was OK with my plan. I was totally unprepared for His answer: "I want you to tell them that if they don't love the prostitutes, I can't honor their church in the city." I thought, "Wow, that's a great word ... for Randy to share ... but not me!" But God made it clear that was His word for this church.

I looked through the bus window and watched as we passed prostitute after prostitute, after prostitute. In that moment, God gave me His heart for them. In every one of their faces I saw the face of my own precious little six-year-old daughter. It broke my heart.

Later, at the church, an awesome worship time led up to the moment that I was to share. When I got up, I read from John 12 and shared about Mary anointing Jesus' feet at Bethany. And then I began to stall. But compassion was rising up in me, and then I felt the Lord say, "Get on with it!" So I blurted it out. "This is what God told me for your church. God said that if you don't love the prostitutes, He can't honor your church in this city."

As soon as I spoke God's word, about half of the church membership got up, came to front, fell to the ground and began to weep, crying out in repentance. Afterward, the pastor explained to me what had happened. Just the week before, they had held a vote regarding buying five homes to use as safe houses for prostitutes, but it was voted down by 51 percent. The people who came forward that night were all those who had voted against it.

I watched as we passed prostitute, after prostitute after prostitute. In that moment, God gave me His heart for them. In every one of their faces I saw the face of my own precious little six-year old daughter.

That very night they called the realtor and were still able to buy the houses. Those houses, surrounding the church, now serve as safe houses for prostitutes.

From that day on, God sent me on a heart-changing journey. He called my wife and me to serve the people of Brazil, saying, "I'm giving you new clarity and love for these people." Ever since, I have loved every Brazilian as my own son or my daughter.

Father's Heart

I began to visit Brazil more often as we prepared to move there and establish a Global Awakening School of Supernatural Ministry. There was no doubt that a lot of supernatural ministry was needed on those streets so that people would be saved. Miracles, signs and wonders would surely help this happen, so I began to press in to receive more faith for miracles, signs and wonders – and they began to happen!

One day, we were in Curitiba and we were going to go out in the streets to minister to the prostitutes, the transvestites and the homeless. Once again I was praying, "God, I want to have more faith. I want to have more faith."

I was not prepared for God's answer. "If you let your faith increase to a level above your love, you are dangerously close to My saying to you, 'Depart from Me, I never knew you!'" My heart was taken aback! I immediately felt a combination of the Father's heart and the fear of the Lord.

Yes, we should press in for faith, and faith is so important, but anything we do apart from the heart of Father is an illegitimate experience. If we operate in faith without compassion and love, then we're missing the point. Think of those people in Matthew, chapter 7, who came to Jesus saying, "We healed the sick in Your name, we cast out the demons in Your name," but they did it without taking hold of His heart.

The compassion/love part is something for which I have to contend. The closer we get to the heart of the Father, the more we will be filled with His heart. This is a lesson I am still learning!

One night we were in a small church in Goiania where my friend Max was leading a healing service. We had such a powerful time as God's healing touch poured into the room. Personally, I saw 23 people healed of noticeable illnesses – spines were straightened, necks were aligned, crippled limbs and joint ailments were healed. There was a four-year-old boy who was 80 percent deaf in both ears. I got down on my knees, put my hands on his ears and said, "Julio, Jesus loves you." He ran off and jumped into the arms of his mother, who then said, "Julio, I love you." Immediately he responded, "I love you, too, Mama," in perfect speech. Wow!

I was so excited to see God work such miracles through me. Then, the next morning I looked out my hotel window and saw a young boy sitting on some cardboard. I went downstairs and took him some water, candy and Pop-Tarts – the only food I had available. I didn't have a translator with me and knew little Portuguese at that time; I just sat there with him. He was so sick that he threw up the food I had given him. But, pool of vomit and all, he and I remained there, sitting together in a beautiful, silent fellowship. About an hour later, a translator arrived and we found out his story. When he was 10, his parents had gotten in trouble with the law and had fled the city. They left him there, abandoned and homeless. For the past five years he had fended for himself, living on the streets. I took him to buy some shoes – he was so thrilled! A couple of days later, right before I left, he excitedly told me, "I have a place to sleep tonight, I want to show you." He took me around the corner to a dumpster full of nasty waste. He climbed over the fencing and lay there, covering himself with a filthy, tattered shirt. My heart was broken because I had nothing to

> The closer you get to the heart of the Father, the more you will be filled with His heart.

give him. I gave him what little cash I had and simply said, "I love you, but I may never see you again."

As I walked away, the Lord said to me, "Nic, when you prayed for the deaf boy to be healed yesterday and when you bought this boy shoes, it is no different to me. It's worship unto the Father. They're both miraculous and supernatural.

We need to get it into our mindsets that the love of the Father is supernatural, every bit as much as when we see great miracles, signs and wonders. They all come from His love. He does it all because He loves us.

Love Connection

On another occasion, we bought some beautiful long-stem roses to hand out to the men and women working the streets. We also translated "The Father's Love Letter" into Portuguese, printed it on beautiful paper and rolled them into scrolls. As we walked the streets and began handing them out, I was disappointed that, despite our efforts, we were not getting the response we expected. We would get to people, hand him or her the rose, and ask them to describe the rose to us. Then we would tell them, "To God, you are every bit as beautiful, gorgeous and unique as this rose is. You are the smile on His face. He loves you!" and then give them the love letter. Sometimes someone would let us pray for them but little more, because the truth is that they are actors. They are paid to say what others want to hear. They don't let you get deep. So as we spoke to each one, I cried out within, "God, give me a word of knowledge, a prophetic word for them – anything to unlock their hearts!" But for three days nothing happened. Finally, on the third night, we came up to an 11-year-old girl – she had already been involved in prostitution, working the streets for a year. We tried to give her the rose, but she wouldn't take it. She was so drugged out of her mind that she couldn't even listen. As I tried to talk to her, she kept on saying, "I'm not in pornography, I'm just walking around," and then she muttered some words and walked away.

Almost immediately after, we walked up to two transvestites – all dressed up. One was huge, way over six feet tall. I asked him what his name was and he answered, "Gabriela." They accepted the roses and letters, but later when we walked by again I saw the roses torn and tattered on the street. My heart broke. When I got back to my room, I cried out to God... "They don't know! How can we reach their hearts?"

He answered with a question, "What are you doing?"

"I thought it was pretty clear!" I responded.

Then He answered, "All those things you are doing are good, but not what I told you to do. I just told you to love them – I didn't tell you that you needed a prophetic word or word of knowledge to reach them. I just told you to love them."

Then I realized what I had been doing wrong. Every time we spoke to someone and handed them the rose and letter, I wouldn't connect with them or look them in the eye. Instead of listening to what they had to say, I kept pressing into God for a word of knowledge.

So I said, "I will go back, look them in the eye, and show and share love." As I did, everything changed. Many of them opened up, wept, and talked!

While we were talking to one girl, her pimp came and signaled to us menacingly to beat it. But at that moment, the young woman told him, "No! They are going to pray for me!" Then we prayed for the pimp as well. The truth is, if we want to see prostitution come to an end, we must reach out to the pimps and johns, too!

After praying with them, we walked down the street and came upon "Gabriela" and his companion, the two transvestites who had thrown their roses onto the street a few hours earlier. They were with another one, and we offered him a rose and the scroll with "The Father's Love Letter." Immediately, Gabriela told him, "Oh, you've got to read that! It is the most beautiful letter I have ever read!" He pulled out his tear-soaked letter and said, "I have read mine over and over!"

> Our purpose as sons and daughters is to reveal the Father. In everything that we do, everywhere that we go, our identity is in the Father, and when people see us, they see our Papa!

Then I realized that even if they threw the roses we gave them on the ground, if they "got" God's love for them, that's all that matters.

They accepted our offer to pray for them. As we formed a circle, Gabriela asked me, "Can you pray for me by my real name? It is Joao (John)."

Do you know what happened there? The Father's heart brings out our true identity. Masks and facades can't stand in the presence of the Father.

Jesus was a man of compassion. The Bible says that He looked at the crowds and felt compassion for them because they were like sheep without a shepherd (Matthew 9:36).

I have been learning that we must never let fear get in the way of love. We must be a people like Jesus, who in perfect love did not allow fear to get in the way of carrying all our sins and dying on the cross for us. This has become a motto for my life, to never let fear get in the way of love.

One final thought. In John 14 Philip says to Jesus, "Lord, show us the Father," and Jesus responded, "If you've seen Me you've seen the Father." This is our purpose as sons and daughters, to reveal the Father. In everything we do, everywhere we go, our identity is in the Father, and when people see us they see our Papa!

So, as we reach out to the lost and broken on the streets of Brazil, my cry is, "Let them say, 'I see the Father in you!'" Yes, I will continue to press in for miracles. But if we don't get the heart of the Father, no matter how many miracles we do in His name, we will not change the world. We have to be able to reach into the hearts of people, so that when a person gets healed, they will have a testimony with the assuredness, "I am Daddy's child."

And one day, I truly believe, we will see the end of prostitution in Brazil!

Nic and Rachael Billman are missionaries in Brazil. Their focus is on setting prostitutes free, taking love into the favelas (slums or shanty towns), and equipping and serving the church in Brazil. The Billmans moved to Brazil permanently along with their three children during the fall of 2010. To read more about their ministry and find out how you can become involved, go to shoresofgrace.com.

Love is patient, love is kind and is not jealous...

it does not seek its own...

does not rejoice in unrighteousness,

but rejoices with the truth;

bears all things, believes all things,

hopes all things, endures all things.

Love never fails; .

1 Corinthians 13:4-8

THROUGH HER PAIN, I KNOW LOVE

Malina's Story

*T*here are some moments in life that define you. Like a powerful, bright light, they sneak into your heart and create new life so that your heart no longer belongs to you alone. You have borrowed God's love and, from that moment on, you carry that love everywhere you go.

My defining moment happened when I met Jane. She died from the consequences of AIDS shortly after I met her. She was only 14.

Up until then, I never fully understood the strong need to hate sin. Sure, we all hate sin. Sure, it's bad and it's evil. But *hate* is a strong word. Then I met Jane.

She was staying at a small Christian hospice for AIDS patients outside of Pattaya, Thailand. Even though she was 14, she looked less than eight. She was so tiny and frail! She reminded me of pictures I had seen of Auschwitz survivors – she was literally just skin and bones, and her stomach was swollen from malnourishment. Her sad eyes rested in deep, dark sockets and her hair was falling off her little head. She was so weak she could barely get out of bed.

I learned that from the day she was born all she ever knew was sadness, abuse, and tragedy. Both of her parents were HIV positive and she was a tiny, sickly baby with the same deadly virus already in her system. Her mother and father had full blown AIDS, and focused all their strength and attention on their own survival. There were no loving arms to hold baby Jane, no soft voice to sing to her, no one to see that she was adequately fed, and no one to comfort her when she cried out in pain.

There were no loving arms to hold baby Jane, no soft voice to sing to her, no one to see that she was adequately fed, and no one to comfort her when she cried out in pain.

By the time Jane was five, both parents had died and she was sent to live with an uncle. But he didn't care about, or for, Jane. She was just a burden to him. He was an alcoholic whose only concern was to satisfy his own need for the bottle. He would frequently leave Jane alone for days at a time to fend for herself. At times she had to scavenge for scraps of food because he didn't even leave her anything to eat – let alone make sure that she took the antiviral medications that would help boost her immune system! However, in some ways being alone was better than when her uncle was home. He treated the small, frail child like a domestic slave, forcing her to spend what little strength she had on cleaning the house and performing other domestic duties. She often suffered severe beatings and other kinds of abuse.

Because the disease came on her at such an early age, Jane's body never developed. Nothing ever got better, only worse. Gradually she got sicker and sicker. She carried the consequences of sin that wasn't hers. She finally became so ill that she couldn't get out of bed. Not even her uncle's harsh treatment and threats got a stir out of her. Undoubtedly, the uncle was frightened – he wouldn't want her to die in his house! So, somehow, Jane ended up in a public hospital in Pattaya, Thailand.

Jane, by then not only suffering from the consequences of AIDS but also tuberculosis, spent several months alone in an isolation room in the children's ward of the hospital. While there, Jane had practically no human contact. AIDS continues to carry a huge stigma in Thailand. Most people are still afraid they can "catch it" through basic human contact, so when the rare visitor did stop by, they usually spoke to her from the other side of the room, afraid to touch her. Jane spent hour after hour just looking at the ceiling. Even though the overworked medical personnel brought her food and medications, no one stayed to help her eat or supervise that she took her medicines. When they returned to pick up her tray, usually most of her food was still there. She didn't like the bitter tasting medicines and didn't understand why it was important to take them. So she would just discard or hide the pills. Understandably, her condition only deteriorated.

Eventually, a caring hospital worker contacted the director of a Christian AIDS and tuberculosis hospice on the outskirts of Pattaya and asked if they would take the frail, dying child. This was where a group of us found her a short time later during an outreach of one of our Extreme Love Mission Schools. When we went over to her bed, at first she just looked at us, eyes glazed and dark with bondage, fear, and terror. For a while she didn't respond to us at all. We continued to love on her and eventually she opened up. We prayed and prophesied over her and led her to Jesus. She prayed to receive Jesus with a tiny voice that sounded like that of a two-year-old. Her eyes cleared and we watched joy fill her being. Eventually we had to leave, but I promised her I would return to see her.

Sadly, her health began to deteriorate rapidly. The hospice didn't have enough personnel to give Jane all the personalized attention she required, so the director had to make the difficult decision to send her back to the public hospital. This is where I found her the next time I went to visit her – once again, totally alone in an isolated room.

For the last month of her life I visited her every week. At that time I spoke very little Thai, but was at least able to say, "I love you" – "Chan rak koon ka." Her eyes immediately lit up and she gave me a smile. I realized that this was the first time anyone had ever said those words to her. For me, saying those three words was not a big deal; for her it meant everything.

There was little I could do for her during those visits other than love on her. I took a cuddly stuffed animal, other simple gifts, and a blanket to keep her warm, because the hospital couldn't even spare an extra one. When I asked her what else she wanted me to bring her, she asked me for red shoes and other "girly" things she had never had.

The last week of her life I took a DVD of the movie "Madagascar" to the hospital. I got on the bed with her and we watched it together on my laptop. Even though by then she was too weak to smile, she was so entranced with the movie that she didn't stop watching even when they brought her food.

She had one last request: Would I take her to Central Mall (a popular gathering and shopping place in Pattaya) when she got well? Of course I said yes, but I knew that she was losing her breath, and I was losing my heart.

For me, saying those three words, "I love you," was not a big deal; for her it meant everything.

Jane died three days after I promised to take her to the mall. God prepared me, and I had peace. She had found her way home. I knew that as soon as she arrived in heaven, the arms of her loving Father embraced her and showered her with more love than anyone could imagine. For the first time in her life, she felt warm and protected. For the first time in her life, she had the strength to dance and twirl – in her Papa's arms. She will never have to experience any abuse, pain, or sickness again. Now, she is experiencing unspeakable joy!

But what about the children who remain? Through my short time with Jane, God placed in me a greater love than ever before for the children, and a greater desire than ever to reach out to them. Because *it is for Jane's tears, and all unloved, abused, suffering children, that Jesus died!*

This chapter is by Malina Zlatkova, XPmissions' representative in Southeast Asia. Her passion for children and their well-being has resulted in the development of projects that aim to save and heal trafficked children in the region. For more information about XP missions and how you can become involved, go to XPmissions.com.

But now faith, hope, love, abide these three;

but the greatest of these is love.

1 Corinthians 13:13

WE JUST HAVE TO KNOW HIM
Rob's Story

*I*t must have been jet lag, because I am really not a morning person. Yet there I was on the other side of the world, wide awake at about 4:30 A.M.

I was in Pattaya, Thailand. I had come over to be a part of XP's first Operation Extreme Love missions and outreach school. We had gathered with participants from all over the world to invade this city, known as a hub of the international sex trade, with the love and light of Jesus. I had arrived the evening before, just in time to head into the opening session of the school. After the meeting was over, I got to meet the students and visit with them. And then I was off to bed at around midnight. I had traveled for more than a day. First on a jet from Phoenix to LA, then from LA to Tai Pei, then from Tai Pei to Bangkok, where I got on a bus for a two-hour ride into Pattaya, and then into the meeting. I was beat. I am pretty tall and don't really fit comfortably in plane and bus seats, so I had been awake for way too long at this point, and I really just wanted to sleep. A lot.

I tossed and turned for a while, and then finally gave in to the idea that I was not going to get back to sleep. I was sharing the room with three other guys on our team – all of whom were having no problem sleeping, by the way. So I quietly slipped out of my bed, pulled on a pair of jeans and a T-shirt, grabbed my knapsack, and headed down to the hotel lobby. My plan was to just sit and read for a while. But by the time I got downstairs, I saw that the sun was beginning to come up and it was getting light outside. I am a pretty adventurous guy when it comes to new places, so I figured I would walk and pray until I found a café or some place that was open early where I could get a cup of coffee and sit and read.

I have ministered in red light districts around the world. I am used to them. But I was not prepared for what I encountered on the streets of Pattaya as the light of day was breaking. I had only been walking for a couple minutes when a young woman on a scooter passed me on the street. She quickly looped back around and came right up to me and propositioned me. This precious young woman with a torn dress, messed up hair, and vacant eyes was obviously on her way home from a long night of working in the brothel bars, and yet her only thought when she saw me was that I must be a sex tourist and she must offer herself to me. This happened a few more times as I walked. Sometimes it was young women on their way home, sometimes it was guys who were pimping out women, girls, and boys from taxi stands or in front of currency exchange windows. All I could think was, "Seriously? It is like 6:00 A.M. When does this stop?" I lost count of the number of times I was propositioned or approached in the ten or fifteen minutes it took me to find a café that was open on the main drag.

The place I found was a McCafé, and there was a statue of Ronald McDonald out in front of it. He had his hands raised up to his chin with the palms pressed together. I found out later that this is a traditional Thai gesture know as a "wai" that's offered as a greeting. But to my eyes it looked like Ronald McDonald was out on the street praying, and I thought to myself, "Good for you, Ronald! This place needs all the prayer it can get!"

I got a latté and headed back outside to where there were café tables set up in a plaza just off the main street. As I sipped my coffee and opened my Bible to start reading, the Holy Spirit nudged me to turn around. I put my Bible down on the table and looked just over my left shoulder. I saw a woman at a table about 30 feet away. She had a cup of coffee and was holding a little compact up to her face, seemingly freshening up her makeup. My initial reaction was to quickly turn around because I didn't want her to mistake my looking her way as some sort of interest that might lead to another proposition. But as soon as I turned back around I could sense Holy Spirit continuing to nudge me. Then I felt Him whisper to my heart, "Look again."

I turned back around. The scene was the same, but this time the way the woman was holding her compact mirror had changed so I could now see that the left side of her face was swollen and had a massive, very fresh bruise on it. She was intently dabbing away with makeup trying to cover it up. At that moment, something inside of me broke. There sat a precious woman. Someone who had been created by our loving God to know His kindness and goodness and gentleness, and yet her experience was obviously so very different

185

from that. She'd had a brutal night. She had been beaten and severely bruised by someone who was hard, cruel, and selfish, and her only response was to do her best to cover up the evidence of it all so that she could sell herself again as soon as possible and potentially be subjected to the same or worse.

My heart broke. All of a sudden this place and this mission seemed so much bigger than us, than me. Yes, I had ministered in red light districts all over the world, but this was something so much more than that. More evil. More dark. More pervasive. This was not a city that had a red light district. This was a red light district that was a city. Everyone and everything seemed given over to the selling of women and children to sex tourists.

I felt surrounded. I felt tiny. I felt completely insufficient. And right there on the main street of Pattaya, in front of a McCafé, next to a statue of Ronald McDonald, I lost it. Tears started pouring out of me. I couldn't stop crying, and in between the sobs I choked out a prayer to God. I said, "Lord, this is too much, this is too big. I don't know what I am doing here. I don't know how to battle darkness this size. I don't know..." Then, out of nowhere, before I could even finish what I was trying to say to Him, He spoke to me. It was so clear. So forceful, and yet so very loving. He thundered to my heart, "You don't have to know what to do, you just have to know Me."

In that moment something shifted. In that moment, all of a sudden, I could feel His heart for this place and these people. In that moment I could feel that no matter how big the darkness seemed to be, it was nowhere near as big as He is. He is the light of the WORLD. That included Pattaya, Thailand. And no darkness, not even this darkness, could withstand His light.

I wiped the tears from my eyes and reached for my cup of coffee. It was on the little café table next to my Bible, which I noticed had fallen open to Matthew 11:28. Right there at the top of the page He promised that I could bring Him the heavy burden of this place, and all the heavy burdens of everyone who lived there, and He would take care of them. I took Him at His Word. I grabbed hold of His promise that I did not need to know what I was doing, I just needed to know Him and His ability to love, care for, and transform every life of every person in that precious city. I thanked Him, took a sip of my coffee, and then turned around to reach out to that bruised woman and let her know how much Jesus loved her.

I grabbed hold of His promise that I did not need to know what I was doing, I just needed to know Him and His ability to love, care for, and transform every life of every person in that precious city.

When I turned around she was no longer there. I am not sure where she disappeared to, but for the next two weeks as we did outreach into the city, the bars, the brothels, the beaches, and the streets, I looked all over for her. I never did see her again, but I did get to watch as the Lord reached out through me, our team, and all the Operation Extreme Love students to transform one life after another. People were saved. Miracles happened. Bodies were healed. The Gospel was preached in word, in power, and most of all in love. And it shattered the darkness.

I can't honestly say that I ever really knew what I was doing that trip, or any of the other times I've taken teams over to Pattaya (Now I am blessed to be leading our Operation Extreme Love – Thailand schools and outreaches). But in going, I have come to know Him as never before. There is not one that He does not love and want to reach out to. Not one bargirl or prostitute. Not one mamasan or pimp. Not one ladyboy or young man cruising the beaches. Not one sex tourist. There is not one of them that He does not want to shatter the darkness for. There is not one He does not love, nor is there one that He has not paid for by what He did on the cross. I have seen evidence of this all over the world, but perhaps no place more prevalently than in Pattaya where I have witnessed great darkness but even greater expressions of His light and love.

It is a joy to go to the dark places, a privilege. Because that is where we see Him arise and shine in us, through us, and around us more brilliantly than we could have ever imagined. And, oh, have we seen Him arise and shine! Let me share a few stories with you.

Prah Yesu Rak Kuhn, Khrap!

I think the first two phrases I learned in the Thai language were "Ahaan arroy mak mak" and "Prah Yesu rak kuhn, khrap." That first one means, "The food is very delicious" (I *really* like Thai food). It doesn't come in all that handy when we do outreach, but the second phrase sure does. That one translates as, "Jesus loves you."

One afternoon, a small group of us were walking around Soi 7. This is an area that is packed with brothel bars. The bars in Pattaya do not have front doors on them like we would think of in the West. The whole bar is open onto the street, and the girls sit right out in front to seduce the men to step in for a drink and whatever else they might want.

We were drawn to a bar where there was only one girl out front. We walked up to her, looked her in the eyes, and told her, "Prah Yesu rak kuhn, khrap." She immediately looked down at the floor, and said in English, "No, no." I stooped down a bit so I could catch her eyes again and said, "Yes, yes! Prah Yesu rak kuhn, khrap. Mak mak!" She shook her head and said in broken English that Jesus could not love her because of what she was. Several women on our outreach team gathered around her at this point and began to hug her and declare her value in God's eyes. We watched as the love began to sink in. After a few moments she smiled, but when she did, she quickly put her hand to her cheek as if she was in pain. When we asked what was the matter, she told us through our interpreter that she had severe tooth pain on the one side of her mouth and that her gums were infected. With bold faith we let her know that Jesus loved her so much He would heal her teeth for her. As we prayed a quick prayer, her eyes went wide and she declared that the pain was totally gone. She couldn't believe it. She was amazed. We told her that Jesus healed her because He loved her. The miracle made it real for her – we could see in her eyes that she was starting to understand!

> There is not one that He does not love and want to reach out to. Not one ladyboy or young man cruising the beaches. Not one mamasan or pimp. Not one ladyboy or young man crusing the beaches. Not one sex tourist.

We then shared with her that Jesus could not only heal the pain in her teeth, He could also heal the pain in her heart. She said she would like that very much, and as one of the ladies on the outreach team laid her hand on the girl's heart and prayed, we watched as she was transformed. It looked as if a heavy weight was lifted off of her. She took a deep breath, smiled, even laughed a little, and then told us that she felt so much peace. We let her know that the peace she felt was Jesus making Himself real to her so that she would know He truly did love her. Right there on Soi 7 she accepted Jesus as her Savior. She even let us share information with her about a good church she could connect with, and a group that could help her get out of the sex trade and learn an entirely different way of making a living. Praise God!

On Fire with "Good"

Early evening is a great time to do outreach in Pattaya. All the women are in the bars ready to go, but it's not really late enough that all the sex tourists have begun to come in and start drinking and connecting with the bargirls.

One evening we found a bar tucked back off one of the side streets where things were pretty slow. There stood eight bargirls with nothing much to do. We sat down at the bar and ordered some sodas. As we sipped our drinks, the girls began to talk with us. It became very obvious very quickly that we were not there for what most people come to Pattaya for. I love when the question gets asked, "Then what *are* you here for?" We always say that we're there to let them know that Jesus loves them, and that He wants to make Himself real to them. This can be met with everything from questions to indifference to mocking. When we asked the girls if there was anything we could pray with them about, the most jaded girl at the bar asked in a very dismissive tone, "Will your God bring me *farang* [a foreign man] to love me?" I jumped up from the barstool, walked over to her, and said, "Jesus wants more than anything to bring love

190

into your life that will never fail you, never hurt you, and always remind you of your great value. Would you like that?" She sniffed derisively, but then conceded to let us pray for her. We prayed a simple prayer asking Holy Spirit to come and make the love of Jesus known to this woman – to make His love for her very, very real. All of a sudden her whole face changed and she started talking excitedly in Thai. Our translator explained that she was saying that she felt something going through her whole body; it was like nothing she had ever felt before. She took a moment and then said through the interpreter, "I feel like I am on fire with ... GOOD!"

> She was saying that she felt something going through her body; it was like nothing she had ever fet before. She took a moment and then said, "I feel like I am on fire... with GOOD!

The "good" fire continued to course through her over and over again. Tears came into her eyes. It was the love of Jesus reaching in and touching every part of her. She gave her heart to the Lord right there in the bar, and then a mini revival broke out. All of the bargirls wanted to be prayed for, and all of them were touched powerfully by God. The Lord started giving us words of knowledge about physical conditions, and then healing miracles broke out. By the time the Lord was finished, each of the bargirls we prayed with got saved, and they all knew Jesus was very real and that He loved them very much!

Love Never Fails

We stay in the same hotel each time we go over to Pattaya. It is on Soi 8, smack dab in the middle of all the brothel bars in that neighborhood. Right across the street from it is a ladyboy bar.

Ladyboys are a recognized "third gender" in Thailand. When boys are very small, if they show any "feminine" qualities (this can be something as simple as picking up a doll to play with) they are sometimes raised as girls. They dress like girls, act like girls, and present themselves as girls. And almost always they are raised to be sold into the sex trade. Because of the confusion, misunderstanding, heartache, and rejection they deal with for most of their lives, these young men are often some of the most hardened people we run into and some of the most challenging to reach with the Gospel.

But the Lord!

Every day when we came out of our hotel we always saw the same two ladyboys sitting at the bar across the street. Sometimes we would walk past them three or four times a day, and every time we would look at them, smile, and tell them, "Jesus loves you!" Their reactions were often very coarse, rude, and lewd, but we never stopped believing that Jesus' love could pierce the darkness, reach through the wounds and the hurt, and touch them deep in their hearts. Time and time again we would see them, and time and time again we would tell them, "Jesus loves you!" They were often the last two people we would see as we left Pattaya after one of our missions schools. As the little bus full of students rolled out of the hotel parking lot on its way to the Bangkok airport, I would lean out the window and get in one last, "Jesus loves you!"

Over the course of several of our Operation Extreme Love schools, and more than six months, we built a relationship with these two ladyboys. And then one day, "Erica" was all alone and asked us why we were always telling him that Jesus loves him. We simply said, "Because He does. He really, really does." In that moment something shifted. "Erica" let defenses came down a bit. We asked if we could pray with him to know God's love, and he agreed. So right there on Soi 8, out in front of a ladyboy bar, in the midst of all the hubbub of a city that is an international destination for sex tourists, we asked Holy Spirit to reach out and touch this precious young man with the love of Jesus. "Erica" began to swoon a bit and said he had to sit down. He told us that he could feel something like liquid warmth moving all through his body, and commented that he had never experienced anything like that. We let him know that God was making himself real to "Erica" so that he would know how much the Lord loved him. It all sort of freaked him out a bit. He became a bit agitated and asked us to go away. So we did. After all, love is patient.

We didn't see "Erica" that next day. But then the day after, on the way back to the hotel from eating dinner, there he was. When I said to him, "Jesus loves you," he got this very warm, very tender look on his face and said, "I know He does." It was such a different response than I was used to that I asked him how did he know? "Erica" then proceeded to tell me that a few hours after we had prayed with him to know the love of God, a couple ladies from our school had come to visit with him. They sat and talked with him for quite some time, and then shared the Gospel with him. He said that it all made sense to him all of a sudden, and that he had asked Jesus into his heart. Now and forevermore he knew that Jesus really, really loved him.

Not everyone we minister the love of Jesus to accepts Him as their Savior, leaves the lifestyle of sex slavery or abuse, and becomes a seasoned disciple of Christ, but many do. With some, we plant. With some, we water. With some, we get to harvest. It is all part of the process – the perfect way the Lord reaches out to each person. And that's really the key. Trusting Him to reach each one. That, probably more than anything, is what I have learned along the way and what keeps me from getting overwhelmed and allows me to simply approach it all one day at a time, one life at a time. It may take months and months of smiles and kindness and acceptance. It may take an encounter with the liquid warmth of God's love. It may take sitting and visiting with someone. Or, like with "Erica," it may take all of the above. But God's love truly never fails!

These are just a few of the stories of what we have seen the Lord do in Pattaya during our Operation Extreme Love schools. And then there are the innumerable testimonies from the amazing ministries there in Pattaya led by women and men who have laid their lives down to be day-in and day-out expressions of God's love to the precious people of this beautiful city. Ministries like Tamar Center that rescues women out of the bars and the "trade" and helps restore them body, soul, and spirit as they train them in micro-enterprises so that they can learn a new trade and never have to go back to selling themselves. And Mercy Center that feeds the poor, visits the prisoners in the Pattaya jails, takes in the orphans that are left parentless through all sorts of heartbreaking circumstances, and does so much more. And True Friend Church whose teams go out to the streets and the bars and the beaches day after day, week after week, sharing the love of Jesus and welcoming the broken and the hurting into their fellowship.

Sometimes I think back to that first morning in Pattaya, and I smile. Not at what I saw or felt, and certainly not at the abuse that left that precious woman battered and bruised. But I smile at how faithful our Jesus is. That early morning, when I felt so small and overwhelmed, He promised me that I didn't need to know what

I was doing, I just needed to know Him. Ever since, just like in Song of Solomon 8:5, I have been leaning on my Beloved as He has taken me from a place of tears, and step by step led me along a joyful path of seeing Him, again and again, defeat darkness with His light and His love. I am grateful for what I have learned of Him in the journey, but even more, I am grateful for what the dear ones in the city of Pattaya have learned of Him. May they all come to know Him – *because for their tears He died!*

May all come to know Him – because for their tears He died!

This chapter is by Robert Hotchkin. He is a member of the XPmedia team and ministers all over the world. He leads Operation Extreme Love – Thailand, taking multinational teams into Thailand twice a year to share the Father's love. To learn more about Operation Extreme Love and how you can become involved, go to XPmissions.com.

A CALL TO ACTION
Unto the Least of These

"Then the King will say to those on his right,

'Come, you who are blessed by my Father; take your inheritance, the kingdom prepared for you since the creation of the world.

For I was hungry and you gave me something to eat, I was thirsty and you gave me something to drink, I was a stranger and you invited me in, I needed clothes and you clothed me, I was sick and you looked after me, I was in prison and you came to visit me.'

"Then the righteous will answer him, 'Lord, when did we see you hungry and feed you, or thirsty and give you something to drink? When did we see you a stranger and invite you in, or needing clothes and clothe you? When did we see you sick or in prison and go to visit you?'

"The King will reply, 'I tell you the truth, whatever you did for one of the least of these brothers of mine, you did for me.'"

Matthew 25:34-40

Pray! Give! Go!

A Call to Action

*I*t can sometimes be overwhelming to hear stories such as you have just read. The accounts in this book are of those who have been rescued and given new life. But what about the others out there whose silent cries are yet to be heard and whose anguish is yet to be discovered? We do have power to bring light into darkness, love into hate.

Jesus invites each of us to do what we can do. Our "loaves and fishes" do help! That which we put in the hands of the Lord can be empowered to set captives free.

What can you do?

PRAY! PRAY! PRAY!

Your prayers release miraculous, divine intervention into the darkest and most impossible-looking situations. God answers the prayers of the contrite and the faithful. As we call out to Him on behalf of those who cannot cry out for themselves, He hears. He will answer our prayers. *Let's pray!*

In the following pages, we have listed Prayers for Children at Risk and Prayer Directives for Social Justice Missions.

GIVE! GIVE! GIVE!

Your financial gifts enable ministries to reach out to rescue the exploited. It takes finances to rescue and care for these precious ones. If we all do our part, we can do so much more! God greatly blesses and honors the gifts that support the oppressed. Giving unto this purpose touches His heart.

GO! GO! GO!

There are many opportunities, both at home and abroad, to serve the oppressed. If you can love, then you are an effective minister. Reach out! Sign up for an outreach mission.

Go to XPmissions.com to find information on how to Pray-Give-Go.

In the Appendix we have listed all the websites of the ministries who contributed the stories and testimonies in this book. Go to their websites and look for opportunities to Pray-Give-Go.

It is time to activate! Do not delay! Their tears are calling!

PRAYERS FOR THE CHILDREN
A compilation of prayers for children at risk

Prayer of Saint Francis of Assisi

Edited Version for Children at Risk

Lord, cause these precious ones to know Your peace.
Where there is hatred, let them feel Your love;
Where there is injury, may they receive Your healing;
Where there is doubt let them be filled with true faith in You;
Where there is despair let them know hope;
Where there is darkness may Your light shine;
Where there is sadness, let them experience pure joy.

Prayer of Jabez
1 Chronicles 4:10
Edited for Children at Risk

Oh, that You would bless them indeed
And enlarge their boundaries of safety and goodness.
May Your hand always be with them and upon them;
Keep them safe from harm, that they might not be caused pain.

Our Father

Matthew 6:9-13

Edited for Children at Risk

Our Father, who lives in heaven
Holy is Your name.
May Your Kingdom come and Your will be done
in the lives of these little ones
As it is in heaven.
Give them each day, their daily bread.
Forgive them their transgressions
And grant them power to forgive those who sin against them.
Keep them from temptation and deliver them from evil;
For Yours is the Kingdom, the power
and the glory forever and ever.
AMEN

The Benediction

Numbers 6:24-26

Edited for Children at Risk

Lord, bless and keep these little ones,
Make Your face to shine on them,
Be gracious unto them.
Lift up Your countenance upon them,
And give them peace.
AMEN

PRAYER DIRECTIVES

For Social Justice Missions

1. Lord, thank You that You have come to bring good news to the afflicted. You bind up the brokenhearted, proclaim liberty to captives, and freedom to prisoners. I pray for every child, woman or man who is a victim of human trafficking and social injustice. Send messengers to them who will bring Your good news. Give them hope and expectation, and heal their broken hearts, that they may receive their total freedom and wholeness in You. Deliver them from the iron chains of injustice that evil people have bound them with. Set them totally free from all bondages – physical, mental, emotional, and spiritual. May each one come to know You personally as their Redeemer and Father. Comfort them in their pain, fill them with the oil of gladness instead of mourning, and a garment of praise instead of despair.

May they become true overcomers who, instead of living in shame and disgrace, will rejoice in the total inheritance that comes to all of Your sons and daughters (Isaiah 60).

2. We recognize You as a righteous God, and ask that Your Kingdom be manifest in every nation in righteousness, peace and joy in the Holy Spirit. Protect every person who is at risk of evil's snare, and confuse the enemy, thwarting their evil plans. (Psalm 119:137, Psalm 37).

3. We pray for all of those in authority. Lift up righteous people who will only want the good of their lands and who will not be corrupted by money, power or intimidation. We ask that Your light will root out all darkness that lurks in places of power – be it local or national governments, or in other places of influence. Let the righteous arise to positions of even greater influence and authority. Fill them with wisdom, passion and zeal to fulfill Your purposes for righteousness. We pray that the mantels of Queen Esther, William Wilberforce, William and Catherine Booth, and others who fought for justice and mercy fall upon your select instruments today, to bring freedom, justice and change to society. (1 Timothy 2:1,2; Proverbs 2:22).

4. Thank You for every person and ministry involved in social justice missions. May their light rise in darkness, righteousness go before them and Your glory be their rear guard. Guide them continually, satisfying their desires in scorched places and giving them the strength they need to fulfill the call. We call forth protection over them, that You will be their refuge and fortress, delivering and protecting them from all evil. Fill them with your Holy Spirit so they may manifest Your power wherever they go, as instruments of salvation, healing and deliverance. Give them wisdom, insight and boldness to fulfill Your purposes, and abundant favor and grace with those in influence. As they seek your Kingdom and righteousness, fulfill all their needs. (Isaiah 58:8-11; Psalm 91; Mark 16:17-20; Matthew 6:33).

5. Change my own cold heart, Lord – give me Your heart, that I may be filled with a heart of compassion and the Father's love. Give me Your eyes to see what You see, an attentive ear and willing heart to hear and do that which you have designed me to do, either as an intercessor, a giver, or an instrument who personally goes.

6. Above all, dear Father, we ask that Your glory fill the earth. We call forth revivals and spiritual awakenings that will bring total transformation to individuals, cities and nations. We thank You for revivals such as the Great Awakenings of the early 1800s, the revivals in England through the Salvation Army in the late 1800s, the Welsh Revival in 1904 and others. Each of these reminds us of Your unlimited power to defeat evil, bring forth light into darkness, give life to the walking dead and total transformation to corrupt societies, through your power, presence and glory. And we cry out, "Do it again, Lord, in even greater measure!" (Psalm 72:19; Isaiah 60:1-3).

CHRISTIAN MINISTRIES AND ORGANIZATIONS
Serving in Areas of Human Trafficking, Social Justice and Mercy

This is not an exhaustive list. Most are the ministries featured in this book, as well as a few others. Many of these websites have links to other outstanding ministries that also serve in these areas. Please note that the geographical region next to the name is where the headquarters are - not the scope of where these organizations serve.

XP Missions - Phoenix, USA. (XP Missions is the missions arm of Christian Services Association and XPMedia, under Patricia King).
www.xpmissions.com

Be a Hero - Canada
www.Beahero.org

Cambodian Hope - Poipet, Cambodia
www.cambodianhopeorganization.org

Divine Inheritance - Southeast Asia
www.divineinheritance.com

Embassy of Hope - San Antonio, Texas
www.embassyofhopecenter.org

Hope for the Nations - Worldwide
www.hopeforthenations.com

IRIS - Africa
www.irismin.com

Mercy Center - Pattaya, Thailand
www.mercypattaya.com

Nightlight - Bangkok, Thailand
www.nightlightinternational.com

Samaritan's Purse
www.samaritanspurse.org

Shores of Grace - Brazil
www.shoresofgrace.com

TAMAR Center - Pattaya, Thailand -
www.ywamthai.org/pattaya/tamar.

Unchained Generation - Maricopa, Arizona
www.unchainedgeneration.com

xppublishing.com
A Ministry of Christian Services Association
and Patricia King

To learn how you can become involved in prayer, by giving or volunteering, please contact XP Missions or other links on the previous pages.

If you have questions, comments or other requests pertaining to **For Their Tears I Died** (the book), please contact Cmartinez@xpmedia.com.

To order books, these may be purchased retail at :the "store"at xpmedia.com or xppublishing.com. For bulk or wholesale orders, please contact: usaresource@xpmedia.com. For Canadian orders, please contact resource@xpmedia.com.

Other Books by XP Publishing

Help, God! I'm Broke! - Patricia King
NEW! Leave lack behind and step into miraculous provision.

Simple Supernatural - Joshua Mills
Keys to Living in the Glory Realm of God!

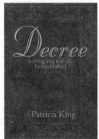

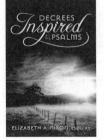